Every Man Has His Price

The Story of Collusion and Corruption in the Scramble for Rhodesia

Charles Laurie

UNIVERSITY PRESS OF AMERICA,® INC.
Lanham • Boulder • New York • Toronto • Plymouth, UK

Copyright © 2008 by
University Press of America,® Inc.
4501 Forbes Boulevard
Suite 200
Lanham, Maryland 20706
UPA Acquisitions Department (301) 459-3366

Estover Road
Plymouth PL6 7PY
United Kingdom

Library of Congress Control Number: 2007940282
ISBN-13: 978-0-7618-3955-2 (paperback : alk. paper)
ISBN-10: 0-7618-3955-0 (paperback : alk. paper)

∞™ The paper used in this publication meets the minimum
requirements of American National Standard for Information
Sciences—Permanence of Paper for Printed Library Materials,
ANSI Z39.48—1984

Contents

Figures and Tables

Preface

At the time of writing, Zimbabwe continues to be embroiled in a seemingly endless political crisis, ostensibly over land, but really about power and the ruling elite's now twenty-seven year hold on the government. For some time I have found it fascinating to see how the land, power and colonial questions never seem to lose their grip on the evocative imagination of the country. Since the year 2000 approximately 4,200 of the 4,500 white-owned commercial farms have been seized by the government, ostensibly for land redistribution to landless black Zimbabweans as a means of correcting colonial-era land seizure injustices. Really, most of the land now belongs to political heavyweights and government supporters, with only a fraction farmed, resulting in critical shortages of food and foreign currency. Hundreds of thousands have been displaced from their homes. Worse, the combination of inadequate food and shelter, coupled with the country's already high HIV/AIDS rate, have left Zimbabwe with the world's lowest life expectancy—34 for women, 37 for men. The government justifies these land seizures and its continuing hold on power by asserting itself as the liberation party that ended colonial rule in the country, the land seizures thus being framed as unfinished liberation responsibilities to the people. Considering that at the time of publication the country will be approaching its third decade since independence, why is it these land and colonial issues remain so resonant?

It can be a poetic indulgence to philosophize about land and territory. Talk of a homeland and reminiscences of the hills and valleys of childhood have a near universal appeal. That said, in some places, as in the case of Zimbabwe, land, power and politics have an especially sharp bite so imbedded in the popular consciousness, they have become something of a self-perpetuating prophecy. They run the risk of no longer being in search of resolution and existing only for their own sake.

What do these discussions of land ownership really mean, and how have these questions become so seated in popular consciousness? Some answers are predictably situated in the recent history of the country, while the more substantive causes go back to the early colonial period of the late nineteenth century. This book seeks to understand this early and complicated period which served such a fundamental role in shaping the second, later time of the nationalist response and uprising. It is this second period that has been more substantially researched and generally understood with greater clarity than the first. Considering the voluminous studies already undertaken on the nationalist era, this work seeks neither to address nor explain it but instead focuses entirely on the lesser understood and probably more important founding period. However, in the interests of providing a complete picture of the scenario, I will briefly outline the nationalist era to provide frame and context for the aftermath of the founding era this book seeks to elucidate.

By the 1950s and '60s Africa was swept by a growing nationalist movement seeking to de-colonize and return nations to indigenous black majority rule. The process, key figures, timelines, and varying degrees of success in each country are substantial topics in themselves, but one can safely say that in each arena the particular characteristics of that nation's history were fundamental in driving how and why the indigenization effort took place. Rhodesia, Zimbabwe's former name, was no exception and had its own vigorous nationalist groups by the 1960s led by Joshua Nkomo, Robert Mugabe and others. At that time black enfranchisement was severely limited. Prospects for substantial and senior positions in government or mobility through social institutions from medicine to education, were generally limited to white Rhodesians. As the nationalist movement grew, the numerous and increasingly militant demands for change and equity were galvanized around the emotive and broadly identifiable calls to redress land inequities. While this was by no means the only issue the nationalists were seeking to resolve, it was a bitterly resented problem stemming from the earliest days of colonial settlement in the late nineteenth century. Predictably enough, it was also one of the issues the white government was least willing to negotiate, for the nation had by that time become highly agricultural with farmers and ranchers holding considerable sway over the government; they were hardly likely to start giving their farms away to anyone. This intractability was especially the case for white farmers who increasingly felt they were the ones responsible for converting unused and often unwanted land into viable world-class farms, and only because of their capital investment, ingenuity and labor of transformation did the nationalists start demanding it back. Nationalists believed equally strongly that the land had simply been stolen and thus all claims of white right and ownership were irrelevant.

It was under this banner of land ownership, enfranchisement, visibility and power that the country's civil war[1] began on the 28th of April 1966 when fifty members of the Zimbabwe Nationalist Liberation Army (ZANLA) attempted to blow up power lines near the town of Sinoia. Their efforts resulted in little damage and all members of their party were killed by Rhodesian security forces. A second group, however, was more successful when they attacked Nevada Farm in Hartley owned by the Viljoen family. Johannes Viljoen and his wife were both killed as were most of the nationalists in the end with only a few making their way back safely to Zambia. While the success of these first attacks was limited, and in fact had resulted in the deaths of most of the attackers, it heralded the beginning of a bloody war that ultimately lasted until 1979 and cost an estimated 30,000 lives.

The conclusion of the war saw Robert Mugabe and his ZANU PF political party take the presidency and become the first recognized democratically elected black leader of the newly named Zimbabwe. The first years of his presidency were marked with reconciliatory overtures toward the white community. He sought to quell fears of a backlash against the former colonials, and took strong steps to assure farmers in particular that despite the nationalist clarion call for land reform, he would not compulsorily seize their land and redistribute it to the black population. Instead Zimbabwe worked with Britain and other Western countries to develop a gradual and legal means of acquiring farmland for redistribution but strictly under the notion of a willing buyer and willing seller, that is, without forcefully and illegally seizing land. The result of these measures was a period of relative prosperity and growth in Zimbabwe, notwithstanding the bloody genocidal crackdown of the Matabele in southern Zimbabwe by the rival ruling party.

The goodwill and early prosperity of the immediate post-independence period soon gave way to increasing corruption, fiscal malfeasance, and dictatorial one-party rule as the 1980s drew to a close. By the early 1990s the nation began to experience serious economic trouble, in part due to severe droughts but more because of poor governance that focused on entrenching party power and enriching the leadership rather than promoting nationwide growth and prosperity. Cleavages between the white farming community and government widened as guaranteed political representation for whites from the Lancaster House independence agreement ended. This was a critical juncture where the interests of the white community and government began to markedly diverge, particularly on the emotive and historical issue of land reform. This nationalist cause had largely been forgotten in its substantive form, except by key members of the black war veterans groups, becoming instead predicable political emblems dragged out at election time to bolster support for the ruling ZANU PF party. This way the party could invoke resonant historical causes to overshadow current domestic problems, particularly the failing economy. In so doing, the government's political disputes with the West, Britain in particular, increased substantially as the leadership sought to blame the country's failing economy on outside forces. In truth, the Western governments had contributed substantially to numerous social causes, especially HIV/AIDS and poverty reduction, as well as land reform. However, corruption and slow implementation of the various programs had resulted in only modest re-allocation of land resources. What was re-distributed ended up producing marginal crops, as the government soon realized that new black farmers lacked commercial agricultural training and the necessary capital. Acrimony between Harare and the West increased as London and Washington in particular subsequently sought to limit aid unless there were anti-corruption and efficacy safeguards in place. The ruling party described such "strings" as foreign meddling in the country's internal affairs.

For these and a host of other political reasons, Zimbabwe increasingly found itself isolated from the international community, particularly from Western powers. In response Mugabe vociferously and aggressively blamed the West for the nation's troubles. He cited with increasing frequency the substantively hollow but still resonant nationalist issues that because of their irresolution – with Mugabe largely responsible for the failure – still held a symbolic sway over the people. More disturbingly for the white population remaining in the country, particularly farmers, the government increasingly castigated them as agents of Britain and neo-colonialists who continued to prosper despite the failing economy.

As the year 2000 approached, ZANU PF found itself facing its first real opposition since independence in the form of the Movement for Democratic Change (MDC). When President Mugabe lost the constitutional referendum in 2000 that proposed the government be allowed to compulsorily seize farmland with no compensation to the owner, a milestone first defeat for Mugabe and ZANU PF, the ruling party sought to entrench its power by sidelining the MDC. The method of doing so was to seize white-owned commercial farms because the government believed white farmers were bankrolling the MDC, and simultaneously intimidate the workers whom they believed were undercutting traditional rural ZANU PF political support. The resulting violence was widespread, vicious, and carefully planned, yet little understood either in Zimbabwe or internationally. Today, virtually all commercial farmland is now owned by the government, divvied out to ruling party supporters and prominent members of the military and police.

The very territory taken by Cecil Rhodes and the British South Africa Company (BSAC) from the Shona and Matabele in the 1890s, argued over by the Rhodesian government and black Rhodesians for nearly ninety years, and the rallying cry for the nationalist uprising to overthrow the white government, is now still owned by a ruling minority only this time it is a minority of ZANU PF supporters. Worse still, and in a bitter irony that only politics could produce, this new minority land owning class are not even farmers. The result has been nothing remotely resembling land redistribution for equalization of resources. In fact, the Zimbabwean economy has been utterly devastated by this move which along with a generally shrinking economy has resulted in over 80 percent unemployment and inflation topping 14,000 percent, the latter a record for a nation not at war. Despite the stated illegality of land seizures by Zimbabwe's own Supreme Court, the government still justifies its policy of complete seizure by pointing to the colonial era policies. Moreover, virtually all actions by the government are in their view excusable, even those blatantly designed to keep them in power, because they are the nationalist liberation government that purports to champion the cause of black Zimbabweans. In this way, the land acquisition dispute of a century ago still resounds in Zimbabwe today.

What this book seeks to elucidate, therefore, is this early and much less understood colonial period. Rather than take up formed ideologies and political rhetoric from the last fifty years at face value, I aim to look back to this crucial and formative period to understand the key players, their ambitions and motivations, the nuances of negotiations between Rhodes' emissaries and Lobengula, King of the Matabele, and the overall colonial landscape enveloping Southern Africa at the time. It is important in the face of fundamental claims today about rights and ownership to at least understand the root of the central discussion in Zimbabwe argued for well over a century. This is not to say the findings will alter the political scene today, for politics defines itself based on present needs, players and audiences. Yet, at a time when all parties blindly point to the past for justification of present enterprises, understanding what occurred a century ago at least gives one the ability to assess the strength of contemporary claims and understand why these issues resonate so fiercely.

NOTE

1. Also known as the Bush War, Liberation War or Second Chimurenga War.

Chapter One

The Charge for Africa

Even today Africa remains for much of the world a Dark Continent, a seemingly endless expanse of threatening deserts and jungles, pockets of primitive warring tribes, lairs of beasts, a continent with a spiritual essence pervasively threatening. Yet Africa has beckoned to Europe for millennia. The phrase "Scramble for Africa" was coined in 1884 to describe a vague period of nineteenth century European imperialism in the African Continent. For the purposes of this book, the "Scramble" spans from 1857 when the board of Directors for the London Missionary Society (L.M.S.) resolved to send a Christian mission to the Makololo and Matabele people, through 1912 when most of Africa was in European hands.[1] The expansive interest in Africa actually began many centuries before the Victorian era when the expansive Roman Empire extended its borders out of modern day Italy north to Great Britain, west to Spain, east to Asia Minor, and south to North Africa. There on Africa's coast the Romans "nibbled," as Pakenham describes it, at the fringes of the great continent with settlements like Alexandria, Cyrene, Leptis Magna and Carthage (Pakenham xxi). Apart from a few forays inland mostly for trade, Rome was not interested in Africa for Africa's sake. Rome was interested in encircling the Mediterranean with settlements to control and expand her European and Asian empire. After the fall of Rome, Europe toyed with and pondered Africa for nearly fifteen centuries before suddenly leaping into what became a dizzying, puzzling and rather embarrassing rush to grab every square mile of the continent.

Suddenly in half a generation the Scramble yielded Europe virtually the whole continent including thirty new colonies and protectorates, 10 million square miles of new territory and 110 million dazed new subjects, acquired by one method or another. Africa was portioned out amongst five rival

1

nations—Germany, Italy, Portugal, France and Britain with Spain taking some of the leftover pieces. A continent virtually unknown a generation before, Africa by the end of the nineteenth century was carved and portioned out by the players of Europe, all vying and haggling through their respective missionary societies, exploration organizations and conquering armies for the most strategic portions of the continent.

By the end of the nineteenth century the squabbling over Africa had poisoned the political climate in Europe by casting nation against nation in a frantic bid for imperial supremacy. No country wanted to be left out of the potential source of wealth and prestige Africa offered. The fighting virtually bankrupted some nations, brought Britain to the brink of war with France, and "precipitated a [British] struggle with the Boers, the costliest, longest and bloodiest war since 1815—and one of the most humiliating in British history" (Pakenham xxi). One hundred years later these fragmented nations of the colonial era have jostled, clashed and struggled with each other to become the fifty-three independent and sovereign nations of Africa.

Within decades of nineteenth century imperialism the inhabitants of Africa were sent reeling from primitive tribal life into the quasi-European marketplace of Christianity, intensive agriculture, large-scale mining, and values as peculiar and disturbing to them as theirs were to the Europeans. For generations before colonialism began, African tribes in central and southern Africa warred amongst each other, conquered weaker neighbors and sought harmony much like the Europeans half a world away. Unlike the Europeans though, the Africans of the region knew virtually no mechanization. Most tribes did not have complex written language. Some had even yet to discover the wheel. To these people, virtually unchanged in centuries, the Europeans surged in with their unprecedented avarice enabled by scientific achievements in the form of steamships, locomotives, firearms and quinine.

The cause for the Scramble remains uncertain. Thomas Pakenham has distilled two "strands:" motives and methods. From Westminster Abbey, Livingstone's tomb beckons to the world, "All I can add in my solitude, is, may heaven's rich blessing come down on every one, American, English, Turk, who will help to heal this open sore of the world" (qtd. in Pakenham introduction). Livingstone's solution was summed up in his "3-Cs," "Commerce, Christianity and Civilization," says Pakenham, "a triple alliance of Mammon, God and social progress. Trade, not the gun, would liberate Africa" (xxii). Answering Livingstone's plea were the missionary societies, explorers, imperialists, patriots, and the prospectors, a mostly British gaggle catalyzed by the call from Westminster to save Africa from itself. And while saving Africa, most saviors and mother-countries hoped to be vastly enriched as well. Africa held dreams of Sheba and El Dorado, of minerals, new rivers, and new markets for "Manchester cotton, Lyons silk and Hamburg gin. Perhaps Africa would be the answer to the merchants' prayers. There might be new markets out there in this veritable new African garden of Eden, and tropical groves where the golden fruit could be plucked by willing brown hands" (Pakenham xxii). Africa also held millions of potential converts. The missionaries, for the sake of African souls, were galvanized and well funded for the venture.

Of course, there was also the prestige of imperialism, an impalpable motive. A weak country in Europe had few muscles to flex. It was hardly likely that Belgium, for example, could grow enough financially and politically to threaten any of the European powers, unless she grew through colonization. She would look to Africa for its boundless territory where her sons could be sent to explore, map and seize resources, human and otherwise, the wealth and power of which could then be played out in political maneuvering back in Europe. While facilitating great potential shifts in power, new colonies also enabled countries to stem the flow of emigrants to America by allowing discontented or adventurous citizens to go abroad, and thereby still pay taxes and serve the homeland.

Heeding Livingstone's call to heal the African wound with trade under the banner of the 3 Cs—Commerce, Christianity and Civilization—a trickle of Europeans began arduous treks into deepest Africa armed only with bibles, a few muskets and what has been called a "missionary zeal," for "not only would they save Africa from itself. Africa would be the saving of their own countries" (Pakenham xxii). In time trading posts were set up, harbors established, churches consecrated, missionary outposts built. As the settlers established themselves and looked at their hinterlands, the Africans soon saw what Pakenham calls a fourth C gradually predominating—Conquest (xxiii). At first the Europeans were far too weak to conquer the indigenous people. They hardly knew where they were. Their supplies and supply routes were unreliable. They suffered from scarcely understood tropical diseases such as malaria. And how could a handful of settlers hope to overwhelm millions of indigenous people, however poorly they were armed? But as they took root and became less dependent on the indigenous generosity and in some areas, their apathy, their philanthropic motivations gave way to a more potent motivation of conquest based upon a curious social movement awakening in Europe—Social Darwinism.

Social Darwinism is the belief that on a social evolutionary hierarchy the Europeans were naturally at the top with all races somewhere below. Some of the supposed evidence for this belief rested upon the many astonishing technological developments of the mid-to-late nineteenth century laboratories of London, Paris and Berlin. One hundred years earlier, with exposure to cultures and technological advances in China and the Middle East, this supremist belief might not have been so easily formed (Thomas 109). Before long, however, the colonial sword was honed with an ideological imperative: the European race was following a manifest destiny of conquest whereby lesser races and resources would take their places, willingly or unwillingly, under the heel of the civilized and omniscient European ideology. "Soon the Maxim gun—not trade or the cross—would become the symbol of the age in Africa" (Pakenham xxiii). Rather than remain the essence and focus of European interest in Africa, Livingstone's ideals in varying interpretations simply provided the moral authority for Britain and other European powers to colonize.

Figure 1.1.   Figures 1.1–1.6 illustrate the rapid colonization of Africa in two generations from 1853 to 1885. Figure 1.1 shows Africa fringed with vague European outposts, a handful of fledgling colonies, and a series of loosely defined kingdoms the length of the coastline. Europe knew virtually nothing at all of Africa in 1853, only that its interior was thought to be a vast desert and its population was thought to be entirely depraved and uncivilized.

Figure 1.2.   A detail of the 1853 map of Africa showing the relatively small British claim to the southern tip of Africa known as the "Cape Colony." By 1853 the British, Boers, some French Huguenot refugees, and other Europeans were established enough in the Cape Colony to start moving north and east to seek better farmland. British interest in the Cape by this time was limited to proselytizing, exploration, and perhaps most important of all, as a strategic gateway for virtually all trade with Asia.

Figure 1.3. The extent of British holdings by 1877. The once fledgling Cape Colony was now firmly established with growth stretching far north into the African interior. By 1877 the Cape Colony was far more than just a colonial novelty, an exploration and supply base or a gateway to the profitable Indian and Asian trade. The Cape was also the gateway to the Northern Cape Colony and Transvaal where the world's richest diamond mine at Kimberley had been discovered.

Figure 1.4.   A detail of the 1877 map, illustrating the segmentation of southern Africa into Boer and British states. The British possessed the Cape Colony, while Natal, the Orange Free State and Transvaal belonged to the separatist Boers.

Figure 1.5.   The colonization of Africa by 1885. Virtually the entire continent is claimed by one European nation or another, with
the exception being most of the Sahara Desert in the far north.
The British have cleverly aligned themselves to not only control
the two main trade routes to Asia via the Cape and the Suez
Canal, but by 1885 they began to colonize a swath of territory
right through the middle of the continent from the Cape to Cairo.
The Cape-to-Cairo passage was intended to expand the British
Empire throughout Africa by providing a means of hauling goods
and conducting trade, moving soldiers, supplying settlers, providing communication, and otherwise establishing a means of control and governance throughout the continent.

   Also clearly visible by 1885 are the German and Portuguese
colonies in southern Africa. These colonies served to frustrate
British imperialism and inflame Anglo-Boer relations with the
fear the Boers and Germans might ally themselves to block
British northward movements.

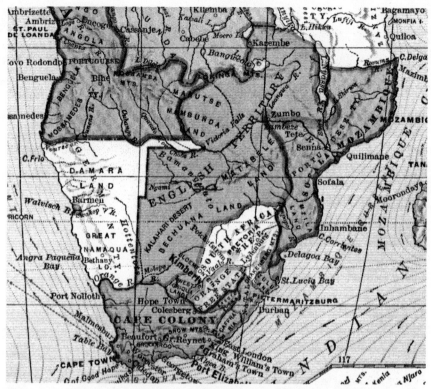

Figure 1.6.   The Southern African power struggle. The British were gradually enveloping the entire southern continent by 1885, even taking land from the hardy Boers. The Boers still retained control of the Orange Free State and Transvaal, but by 1885 any thoughts of blocking British movements north with a German alliance was a distant memory. The British had taken over Matabeleland, Bechuanaland and were close to colonizing a channel of territory from the Cape to Mombassa. By 1885 there were hardly any independently controlled African states. Indigenous populations were nearly all absorbed into the new European colonies.

A BRIEF HISTORY OF SOUTH AFRICA

On April 6, 1652 Jan van Riebeeck sailed into Table Bay on the southern tip of Africa with a charge from the Dutch East India Company to clear land, build a fortification, plant gardens and trade with the indigenous Khoisan.[2] The Dutch East India Company wanted a respite for sailing ships traveling to and from India around the treacherous Cape Horn. This first simple earthen fort and vegetable garden marked the beginning of European settlement in Southern Africa, and was the seed of African land wrangling lasting to this day. Within five years Europeans from the fort took their discharge and began settling land in the vicinity, just a few acres at a time, but acres arcing further and further out from Table Bay until soon the nomadic Khoisan found themselves nudged from their homelands. The uprooted Khoisan then displaced the San.[3] The San moved farther away to inhabit new lands. The ripple effect of land displacement in southern Africa had begun.

By 1688 a steady stream of French Huguenot refugees from the revocation of the Edict of Nantes arrived in the Cape of Good Hope. These settlers embodied, by their very arrival, a spirit of defiance and strength of character ideal for colonial life: "The French added almost 200 settlers, and they brought a heritage of rebellion against oppression" (Morris 20). Along with the Dutch and newly arrived Huguenot's were the English who keenly understood the importance of the strategic Cape in emerging global trade. Within a century of Jan van Riebeeck's arrival, the English had taken control of Cape Town and the Huguenots were absorbed into the Dutch population, yielding a new race called the Boers (farmers), a fiercely independent and autonomous people who soon chafed at English rule.

Farms at the time were usually 6,000 acres in size. Many farmers wanted two farms, one for winter and a second for summer crops. With the arrival of more and more farmers from Europe, the need for land prompted displacement of even more indigenous people farther away from Cape Town. This movement of settlers away from the Cape had as much to do with land as it did with a breathing space for the Boers who took pride in their autonomy and self-sufficiency, traits incompatible with constraining British law. It was said if a Boer could ride his horse all day in any direction without seeing another person, that was almost enough space. They saw themselves as a fiercely independent people; the British saw them as mere subjects. For five generations they "oozed," as Morris calls it, eastward away from the British at the Cape pushing the Khoisan and Bushmen ahead of them like debris on a tide, absorbing and detribalizing while displacing others until the tide abruptly stopped at the Great Fish River. There on the banks of the river the Boer tide came face to face with the not-so-moveable "Kaffirs," the Bantu people (23).[4]

For a time the Great Fish River was to the Boers what the English Channel is to the English and the Atlantic to the Americans, a geographical boundary maintaining with varying degrees of success the impression of splendid isolationism. For the Boers and the Bantu the river was less a formidable boundary than a circumstantial point where not only the tides of distinct peoples collided, but where Europe effectively ran headlong into Southern Africa. While the Boers radiated out from the Cape, some of the Nguni groups (known collectively as the Bantu), the Mtetwa, the Lala, the Debe, settled in Natal while the Xhosa and Ntungwa spread south to the Great Fish River. "It was, in fact, the last free movement, and therein lies the Bantu tragedy. History had offered them a continent, and had given them 10,000 years to fill it, and they had dallied a little too long" (Morris 26). If the African movements had reached farther down the coast, as they possibly would have done in several more generations, there would not have been room enough for the Boers to establish themselves. But the Nguni had not moved far enough south thereby allowing the Boers to scratch out a toehold around Cape Town by displacing the far less militaristic and physically weaker San and Khoisan.

The first meetings between the Boers and Nguni were cautious but curious. The Boers recognized that these people were not like other indigenous tribes encountered thus far. The Nguni were much taller and broad shouldered, a physically powerful people displaying notable courage, fearlessness and defiance of the Boers and their technology. They had only seen the occasional European, usually a shipwrecked mariner washed up on the shore, half drowned, starving, lost—hardly a sight to intimidate or threaten. Yet the Boers were organized, flourishing, and consuming land at an alarming rate in the direction of their territory. As the Nguni appeared far more willing to fight for their land, and fight fiercely, a violent collision of cultures and technology was inevitable. For the Boers, the "Kaffir problem" of indigenous people and land ownership had just begun; for the Bantu, the first instance of aggressive land acquisition by whites was taking place.

THE ZULU CLAN: THE PEOPLE OF THE HEAVENS

In the closing years of the Eighteenth Century, long before the colonial era began in earnest, there took place in the Mtetwa clan, one of the Nguni groups, an ascendancy struggle. Godongwana, the wounded son of the Mtetwa chief, had sought refuge with the Hlubi people after trying to usurp his father's chieftainship. The fleeing Godongwana promptly changed his name to Dingiswayo, the "Troubled One," spent two years with the Hlubi before returning to the Mtetwa where he finally succeeded in seizing power. As soon as he assumed control, Dingiswayo set about building an empire with the strategy of overpowering neighboring tribes, leaving them intact if they complied as they usually did or destroying them if they resisted, then using their men to build his army (Morris 41). This strategy soon allowed the relatively small Mtetwa to rapidly increase both the size of their territory and the extent of their standing army.

Out of a small neighboring clan called the eLangeni, a boy was born in about 1787 from a disgraced union between the Zulu Chieftain, Senzangakona, and an eLangeni maiden, Nandi. Since Senzangakona's mother came from the eLangeni, marriage to Nandi was unthinkable as it verged on incest.

This pregnancy was an embarrassment to the entire Zulu tribe and most especially to Senzangakona, who as chief was supposed to have shown better judgment than to have had relations with an eLangeni maiden, especially when she was the daughter of that tribe's chief. When the Zulu elders heard the surprising news of Nandi's pregnancy, they coarsely responded that the young girl was not pregnant and that her menstrual irregularities were the result of *iShaka*, an intestinal beetle. When the child was finally born, a terse message was sent to the Zulu elders requesting that Senzangakona collect Nandi and his "*iShaka*."

Nandi was quietly made the third queen of the Zulu, and Shaka, as the boy was aptly named, was reluctantly acknowledged as the chieftain's son. For six years as Nandi lived with the Zulu, her fiery personality was constantly at odds with her husband and adoptive tribe causing the young queen to be moved from *kraal*[5] to kraal in an attempt to keep peace. One day while working as a herd boy, the young Shaka lost one of the chief's goats. The resulting spat was too much for the chief who sent his wife and son back to the eLangeni. There she soon found herself and Shaka even more unwelcome, for her return required the eLangeni to reimburse the substantial *lobola* (brideprice) to the Zulu thus causing considerable hardship for the clan. Nandi and Shaka were now outcasts even in their own tribe.

To add to Shaka's childhood woes, he had undersized genitals that could not be hidden since small herd boys were forbidden to wear even a loin cloth. The young boy grew up alone, belittled and estranged from both the eLangeni and Zulu, a tormented childhood that brewed in the boy a hatred for people and seething ambition for power. Near outcasts, Nandi and Shaka moved from clan to clan seeking refuge. The two wandered until the young Shaka emerged from his awkward youth into the figure of a fighting man as an unusually robust warrior of 6'3" in height with a build to match. The young Shaka was said to be so physically powerful and brave he killed a black mamba, Africa's swiftest and most deadly snake, and to have treed a leopard. For these courageous acts he was awarded his first head of cattle. Soon the eLangeni and Zulu wanted Shaka back; small tribes could not afford petty malice if it meant losing so skilled a warrior. Because the heirs for the two tribes had already been established, Shaka refused to return to either the eLangeni or Zulu, choosing instead to fight for Dingiswayo of the Mtetwa clan in the *iziCwe* regiment.

In the iziCwe his years of frustrations and anger were finally vented. Moreover, through battle his political philosophy began to take form. Where Dingiswayo saw combat as an unfortunate but inevitable necessity when palaver failed, Shaka saw it as the one safe and sure method of political growth. For example, Dingiswayo would at once accept submission from an enemy clan and restrain his regiments from further bloodshed, whereas Shaka saw an undefeated clan left temporarily in peace could always turn on a paramount chieftain in a more propitious season (Morris 47). By substituting moderation and diplomacy for battlefield domination, a revolutionary shift in the manner of southern African chieftainship was taking place.

Shaka was sowing the seeds of the aggressive ruler not easily placated by power and wealth. He was conceiving the concept of a new and revolutionary idea for a southern African state, a new worldview based on imposing order and total domination over surrounding tribes to form a kingdom of unparalleled military sophistication, expansionism and prowess. He found in war a method for executing his political ambition. Moreover, and quite unexpectedly, he would also forge through conquest the futures of Britain, South Africa and present day Zimbabwe, this all before any substantial movement of settlers had even arrived on the continent.

On the field Shaka scoffed at tradition. He considered the throwing spear nearly worthless since once the weapon was thrown the warrior was without protection and offensive tools. In its place he forged the *iklwa*,[6] a spear with a shortened haft and large broad blade held continuously by the warrior as a stabbing weapon, and thrust in conjunction with his new idea of a full body-length ox-hide shield. Shaka's revolutionary offensive strategy was for the warrior to lunge forward with his large shield hooking the small enemy shield, then with a quick upward motion lift the enemy shield away thereby exposing the abdomen to a swift thrust of the iklwa. For each kill Shaka would shout out, *Ngadla!* (I have eaten). This style of orchestrated, deliberate and carefully commanded warfare was entirely new to the region and would have revolutionary and disastrous consequences for the more simplistic and often agrarian neighboring clans. Many of these groups scarcely thought about war in this way, let alone knew how to protect themselves from this kind of warfare.

Shaka was a practical soldier. He ordered his men to discard their clumsy ox-hide sandals, dispense with anything not immediately essential in battle, then he marched them over stony and thorny ground for days at a time to toughen both their feet and resolve. Any man collapsing from wounds or exhaustion was immediately executed. Tradition in the region held that warring armies would amass on a battlefield, then regiments would emerge to fight leaving most of the army behind to await the outcome of the smaller skirmishes. When large armies did fight *en masse*, there was usually little strategy involved, just a horde of quasi-disciplined soldiers colliding in a tangle of spears and warriors leaving their nerve and numbers to determine the outcome. Shaka organized his regiments to fight in the formation of the horns of a buffalo, where the oldest and most experienced fighters made up the "chest" and "loins" while the younger, faster warriors made up the "horns" of the Zulu formation (see Figure 1.7). The chest and loins of Shaka's *impi* (army) would meet an enemy head-on, providing sheer bulk and force to hold the enemy soldiers. Fast-moving horns would then swiftly encircle the sides and rear of the enemy causing panic and fighting on all fronts. As the surrounded enemy found its lines broken and chaos breaking out within their ranks, a rout would normally ensue. In this way, clan after clan fell before the discipline, tactics and ferocity of the Zulu army.

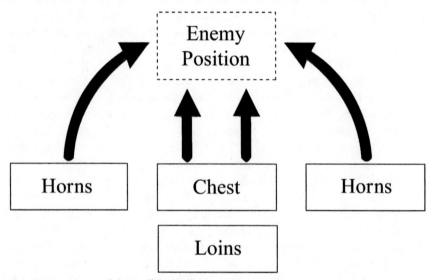

Figure 1.7.   Horns of the Buffalo Battle Formation.

With his army honed, Shaka campaigned to enlarge the Zulu clan by conquering neighboring tribes one after another until the "People of the Heavens" dominated the Natal region. As each clan was crushed or expelled, some were absorbed into the Zulu nation while others fled triggering a domino effect of fleeing tribes surging into each other known as the *mfecane*, "the crushing" (Blake 15). The successor to the mfecane was the *difiqane*, "forced migration," in which tribe after tribe either freshly mauled or facing imminent attack moved away from the Zulu onslaught in a wandering Diaspora of 50,000 people known as the Mantatee Horde. This Horde in turn moved through the region crushing, pillaging and displacing those tribes in front of them, heightening the misery and increasing the numbers of fragmented clans swirling through the foothills of Natal.

THE MATABELE: RISING HEGEMONY OF ZIMBABWE

In 1822 one of Shaka's ablest generals was a minor chieftain known as Mzilikazi. One day, after seizing cattle in a raid, Mzilikazi brazenly refused to send the herd of captured animals to King Shaka as was the custom, opting instead to give only a few head in token recognition of his king. To most chieftains, this slight would not go unpunished; to Shaka, the offense was unthinkable. Knowing that in time an army would be sent to punish him, Mzilikazi gathered his clan and fled north with about thirty followers, fighting and absorbing the conquered tribes in his path as was now the custom in the greater Zulu army. Conquest rapidly swelled the ranks of Mzilikazi's clan, soon known as the Matabele, to where in time he commanded a small army. The name "Matabele" describes well the fearsome reputation this tribe soon earned:

> Already in 1825 Mzilikazi's people were being spoken of as the Matabele, the fearsome aggressors, who carried immense oxhide shields behind which they "sank out of sight" (*-tebele*) when challenged with an assegai. Wherever Mzilikazi journeyed on his mission of death his approach was heralded by hysterical exclamations of "Matabele!" and when columns of smoke rose in some distant part of the bushveld the Crocodile People [native to the region] knew that yet another village had been laid waste by these fiendish intruders—the Matabele (Becker 66).

Near present day Pretoria he settled and tried to build a Zulu-like regime to dominate the tribes within reach, this while still remaining on the periphery of the vengeful Shaka. Rather than creating a sustained Zulu-type dominance in the region, Mzilikazi was himself soon as harassed and sometimes defeated as traditional Zulu prey: "[The Matabele] found themselves disadvantaged when faced first by the guns of the Korana and Griqua, freebooters of mixed background from the south of the Vaal River, and then by the Boers. Those more modernized men also attacked on horseback, which added to Ndebele vulnerability" (Rotberg 239). The Matabele now faced new weapons, new tactics and white people. He and his people would scarcely have known in 1835 that this combination of weapons and aspirations of these outsiders would continually affect and shape the Matabele people for the next century.

In 1836 while still near Pretoria, Mzilikazi first encountered the Voortrekkers, Boers weary of "oppressive" British rule who had traveled north in what is known as the "Great Trek" to find new lands, freedom from taxation and political repression, and isolation to practice their culture freely. The Voortrekkers brought with them horses, rifles and European battle tactics. With these in 1837 the Voortrekker, Hendrick Potgieter, soundly defeated Mzilikazi in battle prompting the chieftain and his followers to flee north where after various vicissitudes they settled in what is now southern Zimbabwe. There they established their capital called Kwa Bulawayo, the "Place of the Killing."[7] The Matabele soon became the power in the region conquering tribes north beyond the Zambezi River, west into Bechuanaland and as far east as present-day Mozambique. "The Ndebele [Matabele],[8] with their innovative assegais, or short stabbing spears, their irruptive, non-traditional military tactics and formations, and their martial confidence, easily overwhelmed the agriculturalists, who were accustomed to defending their homes with throwing spears and less sustained combat" (Rotberg 239). While they easily vanquished the native Shona and other

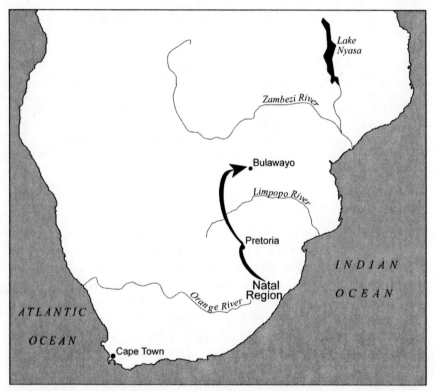

Figure 1.8. The movement from the Natal Region of what would become the Matabele tribe. Mzilikazi first established his capital near modern-day Pretoria, where he established a paramountcy over the far weaker tribes in the vicinity. In time the Matabele themselves were defeated, not by the vengeful Zulu who were too far south, but by the Korana, Griqua and Voortrekkers armed with horses and modern weapons. Fleeing north to safety, Mzilikazi and his Matabele headed toward the Zambezi River, settling in what is now south-west Zimbabwe at their capital, Bulawayo.

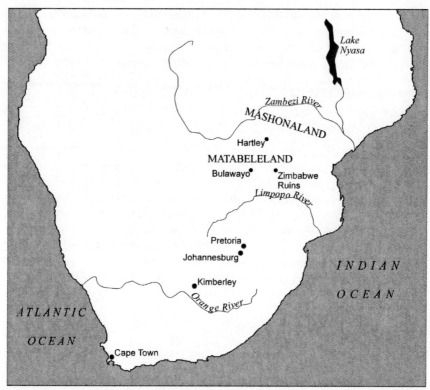

Figure 1.9. The location of Matabeleland and Mashonaland between the Zambezi River to the north, and the Limpopo River to the south. The exact range of both tribes is fairly uncertain. The Matabele were certainly the power in the region, controlling virtually all of Mashonaland and many of the tribes in modern-day Botswana, to the west of Bulawayo. However, it is also true many Mashona had hardly ever heard of the Matabele or their famed impis.

tribes, written indelibly into their legacy was a fear and loathing of the Boers, a Zulu knowledge of battle tactics, and the realization that in times of trouble salvation lay to the north. Soon they would realize that these whites were also interested in moving north.

BRITISH INTEREST IN SOUTHERN AFRICA

Livingstone's Cambridge University address on December 5, 1853 struck a chord of British manifest destiny. "I beg to direct your attention to Africa," Livingstone implored. "I know that in a few years I shall be cut off in the country, which is now open: Do not let it be shut again! I go back to Africa to try to make an open path for commerce and Christianity; do you carry out the work which I have begun. *I leave it with you!*" (qtd. in Pakenham 1). Britain seized Cape Town from the Dutch in 1793, an obvious move for such a powerful maritime nation wanting to protect trade routes to India and Asia. At that time the Suez Canal did not exist. Trade with the Orient took either the highly treacherous and lengthy route around the Americas, or the shorter, equally treacherous, route around the Cape of Good Hope. To control the Cape was to control the gateway to the Orient, and yet commerce was not the only reason for British interest in Southern Africa. Britain—almost singularly—answered Livingstone's call to "illuminate" Africa by sending expedition after expedition to explore, map and missionize as much of the continent as possible. These forays laid the groundwork to make palpable Livingstone's plea, and preferably all before any other European powers were alerted to the immense potential of Africa. Thus, Britain felt a sense of ownership of the continent, a feeling that would in time be aggravated when Europe stirred to the vast potential wealth and prestige this new land offered.

Until the completion of the Suez Canal in 1869, the only two trade routes with Asia were around the Cape Horn to the west, or the Cape of Good Hope to the east. Sailing the western route around the Cape Horn was not only far longer than the eastern route, but was highly treacherous, costing the lives of hundreds of sailors and the loss of tens of thousands of tons of precious cargo. Although shorter, the eastern route had to pass around the Cape of Good Hope, arguably the most perilous body of water commercially navigable anywhere in the world. The Suez Canal, however, enjoyed not only the short distance from Asia crucial for profitable trade, cheaper goods, and

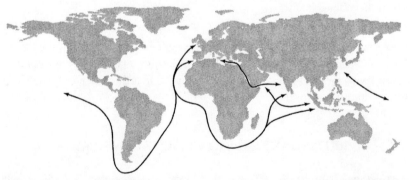

Figure 1.10.   The world trade routes in the 1880s. The route around the Cape Horn was far longer than around the Cape of Good Hope. The shortest, safest and most economical route was through the Suez Canal.

commerce in more perishable commodities, the route was also safe for ships of almost any size.

While Britain was securing her maritime gateways, converting indigenous people and exploring and pegging as much of the continent as possible, the defining moment of South African history was about to take place in an area most thought barely fit for habitation. Quite unexpectedly in 1869 on the bank of the Orange River, a child playing noticed a large pebble glinting in the sun. The boy took the stone home, showed it to his father who out of plain curiosity took it to a mineralogist friend in Cape Town. The stone turned out to be a 21-carat diamond. Word leaked out and the diamond rush was on. In 1871, diamonds were discovered on the de Beer's brothers' farm, Vooruitzigt, near Bultfontein. Unable to stop the horde of prospectors, the brothers sold their property for 6,000 pounds sterling, a bargain for the purchasers when it was soon found that the farm stood atop the world's richest diamond mine, first called New Rush then Kimberley. With the discovery of diamonds, the Cape emerged from being a convenient geographical outpost midway between the treasures of Asia and the markets of Europe, to a crucial strategic possession conveniently guarding both the world's most important trade route and the world's richest diamond mines in the heart of South Africa.

By controlling the Cape of Good Hope the British enjoyed strategic advantages useful in exerting political leverage in southern Africa, the Orient and much of Europe by maintaining trade monopolies on spices, diamonds, silk and other commodities. Their monopoly would not last for long, however. In 1854 the French engineer and diplomat, Vicomte Ferdinand Marie de Lesseps, succeeded in gaining the support of the Egyptian viceroy, Said Pasha, to build a canal from the Red Sea to the Mediterranean. By 1869 using revolutionary new cutting tools and advanced engineering of the day the channel was cut. Not merely an engineering marvel, the Suez Canal severed Britain's precious trade monopoly with Asia and gave the French and Egyptians control over the shortest and safest trade route east. The British would not allow this usurpation of their monopoly to stand, however. In 1875, through a brilliant piece of theatrical finagling, the British purchased all Egyptian shares of the Suez Canal from a cash-strapped Khedive right from under the nose of the dawdling French, thereby giving England a controlling share of the waterway and all shipping within. This extraordinary stroke of economic theater caught the French entirely off guard and gave the British direct control over canal. The British now controlled the *two* eastern maritime routes. Moreover, since the western route around South America was so long and dangerous, they effectively held a monopoly over Eastern trade. Excitement over the Suez was so engrossing they almost forgot the Cape. The British statesman and High Commissioner, Sir Alfred Milner warned in 1885:

It would be simply disastrous if we turned our whole attention to the Suez route to the neglect of the Cape route, a route commanded by no other Power, dependent upon no delicate piece of engineering, but open sea all the way, a broad and safe high road for the greatest of maritime nations. It is not to Egypt, but to the Cape Colony, not to Gibraltar and Malta and the Suez, but to St. Helena and Simon's Bay and Mauritius that we should turn our attention, in view of the defense of our Indian and Australasian possessions (qtd. in Mutambirwa 17).

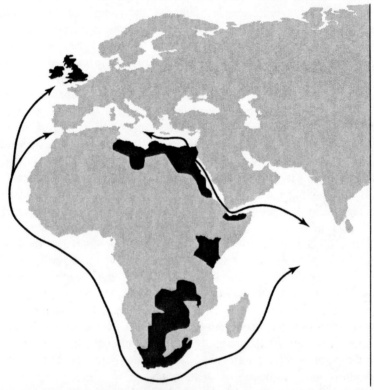

Figure 1.11. Britain's masterful control of eastern trade. By means of providing the few safe ports in Southern Africa for damaged ships and weary sailors, Britain reaped millions of pounds sterling in profits from European trade with Asia. Moreover, their navy, then the most powerful, allowed London inestimable bargaining power over other European powers who could be threatened at any moment with a naval blockade of Asian trade.

This figure also illustrates the almost total control the British had over Eastern trade even once the Suez Canal was built in 1869. French control lasted six years before the British established a trade monopoly with the East. In time the British cleverly seized a majority shareholding in the Canal, thereby controlling the shortest and safest route east. With the Suez and Cape safely under their flag, the British were in a position to influence over the European theater and vast potential colonies in Africa.

The British interests in Africa were then three fold: to secure trade routes, to missionize, and to acquire more natural resources.

CECIL RHODES

On September 1, 1870 a seventeen year old Cecil Rhodes arrived in Durban on the east coast of modern South Africa with the ambition to be a farmer. As the young Englishman bounced off the gangplank, who would have thought that in twenty-five years the paths of Rhodes and Lobengula (who succeeded Mzilikazi as king) would cross, leaving Lobengula dead and Rhodes the richest man in the world commanding an empire of over one million square miles (Rotberg 238). In Natal he indeed became a cotton farmer, loved the land and would ride off sometimes for days at a time exploring the country and its indigenous people with whom the young Cecil cultivated an easygoing relationship, often sharing their food and hospitality. Even at this early period of his life in Africa, however, the conflicts between native people and the colonists were emerging:

> In one letter to his mother he considered the possibility of acquiring a piece of
> 'good, flat land' that had already been cleared and cultivated by a local chief.
> The problem (for the chief) was that this land lay within an area already set aside
> for the colonists, 'so he can be turned off and the fruit of his labors turned to a
> white man's advantage' (Thomas 14).

Rhodes' career as a farmer was to be short-lived. Elsewhere in the region, the excitement of mining and prospecting was rapidly sparking the ambitions of new and established colonials alike.

In October 1871 the flurry of diamond fever spread far enough south to lure first Rhodes' brother Herbert, who promptly left the farm and headed for Kimberley, followed shortly by Cecil. Kimberley at the time of Cecil Rhodes' arrival was far from the organized pit mine of the late nineteenth century. In fact, Kimberley was a morass of small claims all bustling in distrustful competition with each other. Herbert staked a few claims, made a fair amount of money, grew restless and headed north to look for gold but not before giving title of his diggings to Cecil. Within months the young Oxfordian began making his mark on the diamond fields. With the premise of reasonable treatment of labor (Rhodes originated the idea of paying his employees in advance), and comprehensive control of diamond output to stabilize the world diamond price, he sought to bring the melee of digging and unregulated selling under control to establish better and more consistent prices for the diamonds. When first proposed, the concept of controlling output to maintain price standards was laughable to a mining community comprised of suspicious individualists who saw their fortunes resting on out-competing their neighbors. For many prospectors, the more diamonds unearthed the richer the miner. Most locals dismissed the young Rhodes as an academic unschooled in the realities of African mining. However, he stood defiantly by his convictions and with determination and clever maneuvering he soon persuaded those in power to take on his recommendations. It would not be long before these persuasions would become unnecessary and he would control nearly all South African diamond output himself.

One day a miner working in one of the hundreds of pits at Kimberley swung his pick hitting a previously unknown layer of rock-hard blue earth. Only a few dozen feet from the surface, the blue ground was so hard the miner thought he had "hit bottom." Quietly he covered the area with a layer of yellow soil, sold the claim and moved on. In time, more and more miners hit this blue layer. Word echoed around the globe: Kimberley was bust. Claim after claim—almost overnight—came up for sale. Rather than panic, Rhodes calmly, as he would later claim, ascertained that the diamonds must have been pushed up from deep within the earth and so were not limited to the yellow surface soil. If correct, the suspicion would mean the blue layer was just as diamond rich as the yellow. Discreetly, Rhodes bought every claim available until he laid title to most of the Kimberley mine. If laws had allowed and there had been capital, he could have purchased the entire de Beers mine for a paltry £6,000! Nevertheless, in a matter of weeks Rhodes succeeded in owning a substantial share in Kimberley enabling him almost total control of the world's diamond output. His diamond monopoly was taking form well before his thirtieth year.

Rhodes, like many other young men, believed he was destined for greatness. Unlike others, through his shrewd observation, tenacity, willpower and a great deal of luck, he was one of the richest men in the world by age twenty-five. No discussion of Rhodes' achievements can proceed without emphasizing a profoundly important incident in his early life that explains the furor of his almost emperor-like prowess, astounding accumulation of wealth, and astonishingly rapid ascent to power in Southern Africa. He had his first heart attack at age nineteen. Forever haunted by the specter of his own mortality, he led an immediately imperiled existence demanding expediency and necessitating (but not excusing) a relentless drive toward his goals. Rhodes thought he could die young at any moment. So threatened, the magnate stacked his agenda accordingly: he felt he had no time to waste.

Rhodes was not greedy for money as so many mistakenly assume. He was greedy for power. Whatever amount of money he had and the power it commanded, he always wanted more: "His wealth was useful to him as a means of power and he employed it as ruthlessly as he gained it," says Robert Blake. "Power to him was primarily the means to a political end, though no doubt like all who are lucky enough to possess great power he came to enjoy it for itself" (35). He wanted more power just to have more power. So fixed was he on grand schemes, whether they be monopolizing diamonds at Kimberley or gold at Witwatersrand, his immediate lifestyle was essentially Spartan. Sleeping in a tin-roofed shack next to the diggings, wearing dusty and worn clothes, he was so strikingly frugal newcomers to Kimberley sometimes mistook him for an ordinary manager. Yet simple acquisition for acquisition's sake, and Rhodes's mortal urgency to accomplish, hardly explains his true and grander aim. Rhodes wanted power for himself so he could maintain and expand the British Empire: he wanted to make the world British.

On February 8, 1870, three years before Rhodes arrived at Oxford to ground his knowledge in formal education, John Ruskin gave his famous inaugural lecture which Rhodes himself cited as the galvanizing force in his conviction to empower England. Before this speech, the young Cecil was energized and ambitious but without direction for his energy, and without a cause worthy to dedicate his life. Ruskin's words defined the core of his career:

> We are still undegenerate in race; a race mingled with the best northern blood. . .
> Will you youths of England make your country again a royal throne of kings, a
> sceptered isle . . .? This is what England must either do or perish; she must found
> colonies as fast and as far as she is able, formed of her most energetic and worthi-
> est men; seizing every piece of fruitful waste ground she can set her foot on, and
> there teaching these her colonists that their chief virtue is to bear fidelity to their
> country, and that their first aim is to be to advance the power of England by land
> and sea: and that, though they live on a distant plot of land, they are no more to con-
> sider themselves therefore disenfranchised from their native land than the sailors of
> her fleets do because they float on distant seas (qtd. in Blake 35).

Ruskin's speech served to channel Rhodes' energies toward the single goal of making England supreme in the world. From his humble beginnings in South Africa as a farmer, to his early days at the diggings with his brother Herbert, to the eventual monopoly of the diamond and gold markets funding the ambitious Cape-to-Cairo "Suez to the North" railway, Cecil Rhodes ceaselessly served to enrich and further the British Empire.

As with all successful people, Rhodes' timing was impeccable. To many in England he soon became something of a god, a man who with soothing success assured England of her divine right of power and her prowess as a nation: "In an age when doubts had begun to intrude as to the permanence of British supremacy, the exploits of Rhodes were a reassurance that the great days were not yet over" (Galbraith 21). Rhodes made the English feel powerful. Indeed,

Rhodes made the English powerful and they loved him for it. They loved him
because he was a doer, someone who did not simply dream but fulfilled his
dreams with a relentless English dedication to the cause of making Britain
supreme in the world.

CHANGING BANNERS OF COLONIALISM

The evangelizing colonialism of Livingstone was a dimming memory by the
mid 1870s when Kimberley and Witwatersrand were flooding the Cape
Colony's coffers with gold and diamonds, making a rich and flourishing
colony out of the once backward Cape. As mining and farming ventures expanded, labor questions became more pressing. What was to be done with the
indigenous people who once lived on the land now appropriated for modern
enterprises? What was to be done about the shortage of labor? Rhodes neatly
summed up these disconnected questions: "When I see the labor troubles that
are occurring in the United States, and . . . are going to occur with the English people in their own country . . . I feel rather glad the labour question
here is connected with the native question . . ." (Thomas 9). For the Boers the
solution to the problem was expropriation and subjugation, sanctioned by an
obscure reference to the Sons of Ham in the Book of Genesis. The British
needed a more credible authority, an authority endorsing both a technical and
moral blank check: Charles Darwin. Darwin's two major works, *On the Origin of Species* (1859) and *The Descent of Man* (1871), gave a scientific gloss
to the question of the indigenous peoples' place in the strata of mammals and
in the new social, political and economic order of the new South Africa. Wyn-
wood Reade, a contemporary author, states: "the weak go to the wall, and the
strong receive title deeds to the future" and "the law of Murder is the law of
Growth" (qtd. in Thomas 109). According to Darwin, then, the law of life pro-
claims that the weak are inevitably dominated by the powerful and adaptable.
The British transferred this template to the colonial life order, thereby ration-
alizing their domination over the indigenous population with an empirically
proven and morally explained natural manifestation of Darwin's immutable
law of life.
    The irony of the British appropriation of Darwinian Theory to explain
colonial policy, is that Darwin's theory is based on the power and adaptability of species, whereas the British (and other nation's) colonial policy was
based on racism, an inherent superiority of one race over another. There is no
scientific basis to racism. Natural selection does not choose between races or
any other large groupings for that matter, but between individuals equipped
with a genetic legacy of adaptation including the infinite variables of genetic

abnormality, to at once further some members of a species while at once in-hibiting others. Subsequent to the Darwinian justification was a tendency in the Cape to view blacks as not only being unequal to whites, but of being so different on a scientifically provable stratification they were unworthy of equal treatment. The "proof" for the colonials that the black population was in fact *inferior* is a crucial watershed from the Livingstone's plea to "heal the open sore of the world," to "promote commerce, Christianity, and civiliza-tion" for the betterment of the African people. "This development was closely related to the issues of land and labor," states Thomas. "As we have seen, blacks on the diamond mine were unwelcome competitors, but essential la-borers" (107). As perception shifts go, this change in attitude was so gradual that for many the shift followed a natural progression justified by the accom-modating religious and social mores of the era.

For the Boers and British, the "native question" was what to do with in-digenous people after their land had been taken, and what to do about the peo-ple who lived on land the British and Boers wanted for mining and farming. The labor question was proportionally problematic to the resources and acreage of land seized. The more diamonds and gold mines produced and the more tonnage farms reaped, the more labor needed for operation. The prob-lem for the whites was how to induce the self-sufficient blacks to work be-cause the indigenous people did not need money. The solution came in the seemingly innocuous hut tax, a tax on every hut in the colony designed to im-pose dependency and ensure (to an extent) a perpetual, albeit eruptive, labor pool for mining and agricultural enterprises. Revenue for the state and a rel-atively stable labor supply—the hut tax was a neat and tidy solution indeed.

In the early 1870s a tax of 10 shillings was levied on every African hut in the colony of Natal. The going rate for a laborer varies between 5s. and £1.00 a month. Provided that a working family had the resources at home to feed, house and clothe themselves for the rest of the year, they could discharge their 'debt' to the White man after only a few weeks' work (Thomas 63).

Moreover, the hut tax allowed the colonial government tentacles into tribal life, a way of gradually tightening the grip on land and culture by imposing suzerainty over once autonomous tribal governments.

Soon the labor problem became a labor resource. Wheatcroft stated: "What an abundance of rain and grass was to New Zealand mutton, what plenty of cheap grazing was to Australian wool, what the fertile prairie acres were to Canadian wheat, cheap labor was to [South Africa]" (Thomas 108). Cheap la-bor was soon as vital an economic factor in colonial Africa as it is to any corporation today, a crucial element of business as closely calculated and monitored as any other resource and cost of production. In *Rise of Settler*

Power, Mutambirwa emphasizes: "As has been stated, the settlers came to Rhodesia not for humanitarian reasons but for economic reasons. In that fact lies the cause of the black-white problem in Rhodesia. To succeed in the gold mining venture, even if the gold had been found in abundance, because of their lack of capital, the settlers require cheap African labor" (27). Clashes over land and labor then, the southern African saga, were driving forces for almost all salient decisions between blacks and whites from the mid 1870s to today.

LOOKING NORTH

By the time Rhodes was thirty five he controlled ninety percent of the world's diamond production from his Kimberley mine. With this immense wealth he now held the means to seize Africa. Rhodes' great ambition was to carve for Britain a "Suez to the North," a great Cape-to-Cairo channel of imperialism through Africa in the form of a railway line owned by the British, running British locomotives, carrying British goods, and perhaps most important of all, spreading the indomitable mark of British excellence. Parallel to this goal was the reinforcement of Rhodes' mining interests. Rhodes assumed that if the Cape and Transvaal held the world's richest diamond mine and the world's richest gold mine, then why could there not be another ten Kimberleys and ten Witwatersrands elsewhere? Much of present-day South Africa had been scouted with no other promising mineral sites found. Therefore, they assumed, new mines must be in a continuation of the mineral vein north into present day Zimbabwe.

There was another motive for moving north tied directly to the mineral monopoly and the Cape-to-Cairo railroad: the Boers. The Boers controlled Witwatersrand, much to the annoyance and consternation of the British government who loathed the thought of them having so much direct control over exceptionally valuable British assets. To make matters worse, the Boers savagely mauled the British redcoats in the First Boer War (Transvaal War) in 1880. To the embarrassment of the British army who were widely thought to be the finest, best-equipped and most modern fighting force in the world, the despised Boer army was made up mostly of farmers equipped with their own rifles riding on scrub ponies. They inflicted astonishing defeats on the redcoats at the Battles of Laing's Nek, Ingogo and Majuba Hill. Fought on February 26th 1881, the Battle of Majuba Hill was an especially vicious sting for the British, not only because they incurred 280 casualties out of 400 troops, but because one of the Britain's most celebrated soldiers, General Colley, was shot through the head in the humiliating rout.[9] Boer power had to be checked

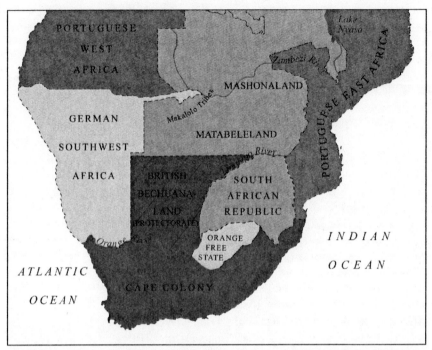

Figure 1.12. The political picture of Southern Africa in 1885. As the British entrenched their presence in the south, they feared the Boers in the South African Republic and Orange Free State would ally themselves with German Southwest Africa. This scenario was most troubling if the political move resulted in them seizing Mashonaland and Matabeleland, thereby controlling the expected mineral wealth of the region and blocking British northward movement. Fearing that the Boers would ally themselves with the Germans in Southwest Africa, the British seized control of the Bechuanaland territory to safeguard their Cape-to-Cairo route. This action prevented a Boer-German block directly north of the Cape Colony. In reality though, the very same threat simply materialized farther north to the twenty-second parallel. Above this demarcation lay Matabeleland. If either the Boers or the Germans were to overrun the Matabele, the virtual countrymen could then join hands and block the northward British advance. By the same token, the Portuguese could also halt British movement by conquering modern-day Zambia and bridging their east and west African territories. It was crucial, therefore, for the British to carve for themselves a swath of territory through Central Africa to preserve their sub-Saharan expansion.

before it spread farther north, for if the Boers controlled the next mineral deposits the financial disaster for Rhodes and the Empire would be substantial.

The British government remained recalcitrant in allowing Rhodes to move north until fate conveniently intervened in the form of Otto von Bismarck. In August 1884, the chancellor seized Angra Pequena (a port in present-day Namibia), leaving only Bechuanaland (modern-day Botswana) separating the German territory from the pro-German Boers. If Boers and Germans allied themselves, Britain's northward ambitions would be effectively halted. With the Portuguese already in the east, a potential German-Boer swath across the North, the languid attitude of the British under Gladstone galvanized to prevent any potential block.

Then there was the biblical land of Ophir. A German schoolmaster turned explorer, called Carl Mauch, discovered what he deemed to be "sensationally" rich veins of gold in Matabeleland and Mashonaland, the known mining sites of the Monomatapa's (sixteenth century African kings who ruled much of present-day Zimbabwe). Mauch soon also discovered the ruins of Great Zimbabwe, a massive and unique site built of carefully cut granite stones crafted into great towers and intricately decorated stone walls. With remarkable alacrity, Mauch announced that Great Zimbabwe was a copy of Solomon's temple in Jerusalem built by the Queen of Sheba (Parfitt 222). After visiting two sites, later to be named Hartley Hills and Tati, Mauch reported, "how the vast extent and beauty of these goldfields are such that at a particular point I stood as it were transfixed, riveted to the place, struck with amazement and wonder at the sight and for a few minutes was unable to use the hammer" (qtd. in Galbraith 31). Evidence in hand, Mauch boldly announced he had discovered the biblical Land of Ophir, where King Solomon's mines were said to be located!

With Witwatersrand and Kimberley so close to Matabeleland and Mashonaland, Mauch, Rhodes and a great many others who read the mining reports were soon giddy and exuberant speculators coveting the riches of Ophir. The "proof" seemed conclusive. E. P. Mathers, a contemporary, noted, "Today, then, the Englishmen is in the land of Ophir—opening the treasurehouse of antiquity . . . At least before many years are out, we may expect to see the image of Queen Victoria stamped on the gold with which King Solomon overlaid his ivory throne, and wreathed the cedar pillars of his temple" (qtd. in Parfitt 224). Self-fulfilling prophecy or not, biblical Ophir beckoned earnestly to Rhodes and the Boers alike. The rush to control the mining concessions there was on.

Hemmed in to the west and east by the protocols of the London Convention, the Boers were also looking northward. The North promised more land which in turn promised the potential of other Witwatersrands and Kimber-

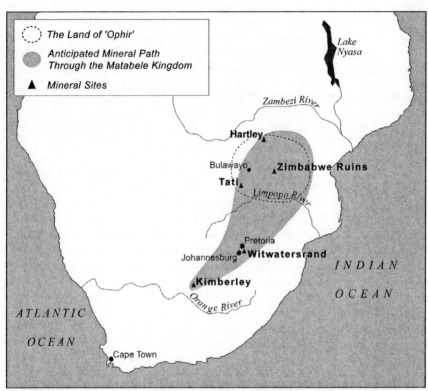

Figure 1.13. The anticipated mineral swath through Southern Africa. Prospectors, explorers, businessmen and politicians assumed that if the world's biggest diamond mine was at Kimberley, and the world's most profitable gold mine was at Witwatersrand, it was a virtual certainty there would be other such mines in a mineral vein running north into Mashonaland and Matabeleland. The rather fanciful and exaggerated "proof" from prospectors of such a swath, appeared to confirm what many thought to be common sense. The unfortunate Lobengula, however, soon found his kingdom in the sights of mineral-hungry men from as far away as the United States. Lobengula could never have known how merely the rumor of gold and minerals would turn the focus of colonial conquest irrevocably on his people.

leys, not to mention closer geographical ties with German colonies to politically and geographically isolate the British. Once the discovery of gold at
Witwatersrand had begun to ease the Transvaal's precarious financial situation, the leaders "could also contemplate adventures that were both specula-
tively and diplomatically bold. Thus Kruger (leader of the Boers and President of the South African Republic) initiated or approved an overture to
Lobengula which, coming unexpectedly, was designed to anticipate and frustrate any similar moves by the Cape or Britain" (Rotberg 248). Like Rhodes,
the Boers found their dreams funded by gold.

The Boers were the first to strike solidly north with a treaty drafted by
Kruger personally and signed by Lobengula and four of his *indunas*.[10] The
Grobler Treaty bound the Transvaal and the Matabele to "perpetual peace
and friendship" (Rotberg 248). The Treaty declared Lobengula to be an ally
of the South African Republic, to accept a resident consul in Matabeleland,
to send troops whenever called upon, and finally, it implied that Lobengula
was a vassal of the Republic (Rotberg 248). Fortunately for the British
and Matabele, the authenticity of the Grobler Treaty was suspect from
the beginning because the indunas' signatures had strange un-Matabele-like
names, and the document had not been signed by any independent white witnesses, such as a missionary, as was customary. In fact, the only European
signatures on the document were those of Grobler and his brother. Moreover,
if Lobengula had signed the document at all, it was more likely the King
thought he was signing a document of friendship, because he could not
read and almost certainly would never have made such sweeping
concessions including the sending of troops to assist the Boers when they
themselves were an old and bitter enemy. The authenticity of the document
is less important than the ramifications of the signing itself. As with Bismarck's land grab at Angra Pequena, the Grobler Treaty electrified the
British into realizing what Rhodes had been saying all along: the Boers
were a real and potential threat ready and nearly succeeding in choking off
the Cape-to-Cairo route.

The Missionaries also looked north. The London Missionary Society
(LMS) sponsored Livingstone's expedition in 1857 when he passed through
Mashonaland and Matabeleland eventually "discovering" and naming Victoria Falls. Robert Moffat, also a member of the LMS, had been proselytizing
modern-day South Africa, Botswana and Zimbabwe since 1816. The goal of
the LMS was to spread Christianity through heathen Africa, dispensing the
balm of salvation to the open sore of the world. Moving north and expanding
already established but sparsely spread missions, Christians could reach a virtually limitless supply of new converts.

For a time the missionary movement seemed in competition with Rhodes and prospectors over new territories to the north. David Carnegie, one of the missionaries who for many years had been trying without success to convert the Matabele to Christianity, wrote, "gold and the gospel are fighting for the mastery, and I fear gold will win" (qtd. in Galbraith 24). In time gold and gospel would become intimate allies.

NOTES

1. The only exceptions were Liberia and Ethiopia.

2. Previously known as the Hottentots.

3. Previously known as Bushmen.

4. Etymologically "Kaffir" is an Arabic word meaning "infidel." Kaffir today carries strong derogatory connotations.

5. *Kraal* is an Afrikaans word usually meaning a small village often surrounded by a stockade. However, the term can also be used to denote a substantially larger and more sophisticated city such as Bulawayo, the seat of the Matabele kingdom.

6. "Iklwa" is an onomatopoetic word for the short stabbing spear forged by Shaka. The Zulu word represents the sucking sound the spear makes when withdrawn from a body.

7. Kwa Bulawayo is usually known as "Bulawayo."

8. Today "Matabele" and "Ndebele" are used interchangeably. There is debate as to the origins of each name. Robert Blake states that "Matabele" translates into "people of the long shields," plausible since Mzilikazi and his few followers were of Zulu stock and the Zulu were well known for their body-length shields (Blake 16). In *Origins of Rhodesia*, Samkange claims that "Matabele" translates into "those who disappear behind their shields," again plausible because of the body-length shields (13). Dodds goes into more detail: "Matabele" is an anglicized version of a Sotho word, "Matabele", which was evidently used as a blanket term by the Sotho when referring to 'strangers from the East' such as the Khumalos who had made their way on the highveld from the coastal belt. In due course, the nation founded by Mzilikazi adopted the name in its Nguni form of "Amandebele", although most modern scholars use the root "Ndebele" instead. In Mzilikazi's day, however, his people used other names to describe themselves, such as Khumalo or Zulu" (156). Although admittedly somewhat arbitrary, 'Matabele' is the designation in this paper due to its near universal recognition.

9. The importance of the Battle of Majuba Hill to South African and Rhodesian history cannot be overstated. With advanced training, modern rifles and artillery the British army was not simply beaten by the Boers at Majuba, but trounced. Of the 400 British soldiers, there were 280 casualties including, most shocking of all, one of Britain's most celebrated soldiers of the time, General Colley. The Boers, on the other hand, suffered two dead, four wounded (Opperman 63). The number of casualties

jolted the British into realizing the Boers were indeed a formidable foe. More importantly, the long-term effect was to shake British confidence and to damage her reputation in Europe and Africa for years to come. Most profound of all for the history of Zimbabwe, the British fallibility at Majuba was to play a significant part in the decision of Lobengula, king of the Matabele, to sign the Rudd Concession, for Majuba Hill proved British vulnerability.

    10. An "induna" was a counselor or cabinet member of the Matabele nation.

Chapter Two

The Fly and the Chameleon

MORAL STRATEGY FOR OVERCOMING LOBENGULA

Before force of arms could be used to occupy Matabeleland and Mashona-land, and even before legal imperialism was brought to the fore, there had to be a moral reason for a land occupation. Warfare for the sake of conquering is crude; warfare for the sake of a moral virtue under a banner of moral authority is righteous, even Biblical. In an era where civilized mankind was seen in an epic battle against depraved people, development and civilization paved a righteous path for the Europeans. "[Rhodes] believed that 'progress' would come more quickly," says Mason, "if Europeans occupied the country, and he did not question the desirability of 'progress'; it was a view that in 1890 no European would have questioned" (126). Civilizing was a moral duty.

> At a meeting of the London Chamber of Commerce in May 1888, at which John Mackenzie was the principal speaker, Joseph Chamberlain expressed baldly the sentiment that less direct contemporaries clothed in idealistic language: '. . . so far as the unoccupied territories between our present colonial possessions and the Zambezi are concerned, they are hardly practically to be said to be in the possession of any nation. The tribes and Chiefs that exercise domination in them cannot possibly occupy the land or develop its capacity, and it is certain as destiny that, sooner or later, these countries will afford an outlet for European enterprise and European colonization . . .' (Galbraith 25).

Therefore, the right of land ownership should go to whoever could develop it most fruitfully. This social Darwinist philosophy did not simply allow conquest: it demanded it with scientific determinism. Since the English defined this development, they naturally saw themselves as being most fit to occupy. The author Percy Fitzpatrick states, "[Mashonaland is] a land, which in the hands of raw untaught savages can produce in great quantity and of excellent quality corn of all sorts . . . must surely in the hands of intelligent energetic men be capable of enormous developments. It is a natural garden and granary" (126). The English, therefore, felt justified in seizing Mashonaland and Matabeleland.

If the natural destiny of civilization to uproot savagery was not enough, there were frequent references to "rules" of absolute power, a law-of-the-jungle judiciary where might makes right. The famous hunter, Frederick Courtney Selous, referred to, "the good old rule, the simple plan, that they should take who have the power and they should keep who can" (qtd. in Galbraith 25). The social Darwinist philosophy gave their actions a virtuous inevitability: they were simply carrying out what would happen at some point anyway. Thus when writing home in 1889, Rhodes said, "If we do not occupy someone else will" (qtd. in Rotberg 290). The motivation satisfied both the polished and rawest of human impulses, the law of nature cloaked in social, religious and political affirmations demanding for the sake of the conqueror and conquered alike the realization of the natural order of civilization.

OVERTHROW OF THE "TYRANT"

In what was painted a philanthropic Christian action, the British established a moral imperative whereby certain tyrannical rulers had to be removed for the sake of those whom they oppressed. In this way the British would conquer Lobengula for the sake of the Matabele. For this justification to be valid, the leader must conform to "the accepted picture of the tyrannical African chief who terrorized not only his enemies but his own people, living in fear of the whims of a despot who might, if the mood struck him, order the death of any of his subjects, or even hundreds of them" (Galbraith 25). Shaka, Mzilikazi and eventually Lobengula were the apotheoses such African tyrants being seen as both brutal and omnipotent. Reports of Matabele horrors had filtered down to South Africa for generations from hunters, explorers and missionaries who witnessed life in Bulawayo and sometimes saw the aftermath of Matabele raids on the Mashona. An account from one early missionary describes coming across burned out villages, near were the bodies of men pinned to the ground with ropes and stakes so they would die in the sun. Near to them could be found women and children, skulls crushed with single knobkerrie blows from the rampaging impis. These reports were undoubtedly exaggerated in many cases to satisfy both the Victorian curiosity about "savages" and their customs, and also the political aims of various European nations that could be more easily undertaken if against a cruel enemy. In this way the British and Rhodes were adequately armed with eyewitness accounts and propaganda to garner public support for the destruction of such tyrannical leaders. Credible missionaries and some explorers, perhaps unwittingly, put the English in a moral dilemma where they in time felt compelled to send an army to expel the tyrant or otherwise be responsible for willfully allowing such atrocities to occur. This moral dilemma served as a profoundly powerful tool for key power brokers and opportunists of the period.

RHODES' ROYAL CHARTER

After the Grobler Treaty was discredited, Rhodes' first concern was to ensure that Britain was the only European power to secure the Matabeleland and Mashonaland territories. Once British supremacy was ensured, he aimed to secure the anticipated diamond and gold monopolies under the military and political protection of the English flag. The first step in the sequence was signing the Moffat Treaty on February 11, 1888. In the treaty named for John Smith Moffat, son of the famed missionary Robert Moffat, Lobengula agreed not to engage in negotiations with any foreign power without first consulting the British. This seemingly small promise had the important consequence of precluding any Boer, Portuguese or German meddling in a massive swathe of land right through central Africa. The agreement also prevented the Boers from pinching off the British, while assuring that if Rhodes did not control the interests in Lobengula's kingdom, at least a British company would.

Once the Moffat Treaty was signed, Rhodes needed a Royal Charter granting him exclusive mineral rights over Matabeleland and Mashonaland. Before he could secure this charter, an agreement was needed from Lobengula allowing Rhodes' enterprises complete control over mineral rights because the British government would never grant the rare monopoly over territories if the native king opposed. The British government wanted cheap colonization not another war. As Claire Palley states in *Zulu and Matabele Warrior Nations*, "While the Charter gave the Company legal capacity and conditional permission from the Crown to exercise governing powers that it might in the future acquire, the Company could only seek the source of its actual administration in the grant of governing powers by the sovereign of the country, king Lobengula" (189). With Europeans out of the picture, the Royal Charter was essential to block competing British interests from doing as much damage to Rhodes' plans as any other European power could.

Chartered companies were not Rhodes' original idea. The British East India Company, British East Africa Company and the Royal Niger Company, amongst others, all provided models by which organizations enjoyed monopolistic control over vast territory in exchange for the responsibility of developing the region. While the costs associated with the charter were so daunting as to bankrupt some of the world's richest companies, the potential payoff was monumental. In Rhodes' case, he was already the world's richest man. Protected by the Crown, the chartered company would enjoy a free hand in developing the infrastructure of the new territory. Meanwhile, the British were waiting in the background ready to step in to raise their flag once the colony was stable and profitable. For the British government, it was colonization on the cheap because the government forewent most colonial responsibilities until many of the risks and expenses of developing a new colony were fronted by the company (Thomas 189). This model of granting the Royal Charter first and then establishing government was far more successful than most other colonizing models.

The Germans and French colonized by first sending troops to establish a national presence, followed by the infusion of business interests to develop and exploit the colony. "Writing in 1896, an American admirer of the British system estimated that colonial occupation had already cost the French $750 million (over £8 billion at today's values), while each German colonist had cost his home government $1750 (equivalent to £8000 today)" (Thomas 189). To the frugal British government with vacillating taxpayers, the charter company seemed an ideal solution. Gann explains:

> To the metropolitan government ventures such as the British South Africa Company offered many advantages. They supplied capital without making demands on the taxpayer; they took risks the home government would not take . . . From the financial point of view chartered companies might in some ways be described as the 'forlorn hope' of investment capital, a kind of 'commando force' which would set up economic bridgeheads at the risk of being wiped out itself (81).

Thus when Rhodes approached London with plans of securing a charter, he carefully laid before the government his northward scheme—a Cape-to-Cairo railway and telegraph lines to encourage immigration, promote trade and commerce, and develop mining—all at nominal expense to the taxpayer (Mason 127). "In the 1880s, with so many overseas responsibilities, so many new demands, and so much caution and indecision on the part of the Treasury mandarins, encouraging private enterprise to extend the empire . . . made excellent sense to everyone in Downing Street and Whitehall" (Rotberg 254). An added bonus was that by securing Matabeleland and Mashonaland, the British would then own territory right in between the Portuguese and Germans, a physical

presence to deter infractions on the Moffat Treaty. Not only would this territory then be colonized by British speaking and British thinking colonists, a
cultural counteraction to the Transvaalers, but the geographic pinch would
make the separatist Cape that much more reliant on Britain for protection
(Gann 81). The government was to an extent behind Rhodes as long as he
could secure the *foundation* for the Royal Charter—the Rudd Concession.

LOBENGULA'S DILEMMA

Rhodes' mission was clear: secure Matabeleland and Mashonaland for the
British flag, protect his diamond and gold monopoly, and maintain a wide
swathe of land for a Cape-to-Cairo railroad. Lobengula faced a far more complex and bewildering predicament. For the first time his people were facing a
different sort of person, the white man driven by astonishing persistence and
armed with overwhelming technological advancement both on and off the
battlefield. Perhaps most daunting and debilitating of all, Lobengula realized
his people were psychologically rooted in a different age. Everyone wanted
his Matabele kingdom. Perhaps only Lobengula, Lotshe (his Prime Minister)
and a handful of others understood they faced almost inevitable annihilation
if they had tried to maintain their current state of domination of traditional enemies with traditional weapons, while ignoring the new European threats.

From the Zulu the Matabele inherited a proud military tradition of offensive hand-to-hand warfare with the shield, knobkerrie and assegai. For fifty
years their tactics proved devastatingly successful, decimating almost all who
opposed them. Their power was so great, their efficiency so honed, their ruth-
lessness so total, the Matabele were known world wide. Even today their
prowess is almost mythical. However, just as armies have done from time im-
memorial, the Matabele soon began to suffer from an acceptance of their supremacy, a comfort with their weapons and tactics, and a banal acquiescence
to their own power. Ironically, the Matabele were soon to be defeated by their
very own success.

Far more forgivable in the slower pace of Africa, Lobengula's soldiers
reveled in a tradition where warriors attacked hand-to-hand with spears and
clubs, proving their mettle on the battlefield. Man-to-man combat where
death and bloodshed were not merely significant to victory, but crucial social and sometimes political coming-of-age milestones, made their obsoles-
cence that much harder to acknowledge for all concerned. For example, warriors could earn the right to marry after showing bravery on the battlefield.
To many Matabele, especially the older indunas, rifles were undignified,
even cowardly: ". . . the whole mentality of the Ndebele military leaders was

resistant to reform. Like the Prussians before Jena or the French before Su-
dan, they were rigid conservatives thinking in terms of tactics of a vanishing
world" (Blake 45). It was this static adherence to proven tactics in a highly
transitional environment that led to the rise of Shaka Zulu and Mzilikazi
three generations prior, and would in time lead to the fall of the Matabele.

By the 1880s the Matabele were no longer the all-conquering warriors of
southern Africa. The Bechuanas had soundly defeated them twice with cavalry and modern weapons. Rifle fire meant the Matabele could be killed at a
distance, thus completely negating the efficacy of traditional hand-to-hand
tactics. Then again in 1885,

> . . . one of his [Lobengula's] *impis* received a crushing defeat from the forces of
> Khama, the Chief of the Bamangwato. Armed with modern rifles, they de-
> stroyed the Ndebele army near the Okovango River. The Ndebele had failed to
> secure adequate firearms, nor did they possess any cavalry—again unlike
> Khama who had some 300 horsemen in his numerically inferior but technically
> superior army. Khama's ascendancy was due to his prudent espousal of British
> protection, and to long-established trade relations which supplied him with the
> weapons he needed (Blake 45).

Realizing this new vulnerability from not only Europeans but now also traditional enemies who but recently had cowered at the sight of an impi, Lobengula became desperate for modern weapons.

Compounding his situation, he knew the real threat came not from the
Bechuanas or Bamangwato, but from the English and Boers. Using similar
tactics to the Matabele, the Zulu won a startling victory at Isandhlwana on
January 22nd, 1879 over the English, killing 1,200 of the Imperial force, by
far the worst routing of the British army in the Victorian era. The very next
day though at Rorke's Drift, a well fortified British force of a little over 120
men defended themselves successfully from a Zulu onslaught of over 3,000
warriors. The difference this time for the British was a change in defensive
tactics. Then on July 4th, 1879 the main Zulu army at the Battle of Ulundi
was wiped from the savannah by a British force which suffered not a single
casualty. Morris describes the carnage:

> Regiment after regiment surged forward, and the lines began to melt away in the
> hail of bullets scything the slopes. Succeeding waves charged over the contorted
> bodies that littered the grass, and the shining faces of the warriors, with gleam-
> ing eyes and set teeth, bobbed up and down over the rims of their shields. Raw
> courage had brought them that far, but bravery alone could not force them
> through the crescendo of fire, and the warriors sank to their knees to crash full
> length in the dust or tumble head over heels in mid-stride. Not a Zulu reached
> to within thirty yards of the British lines (569).

Of course Lobengula knew the British learned from their defeat at Isandhlwana, and within five months had defeated the Zulu. These developments did not bode well for the Matabele being that their tactics where essentially Zulu. Whilst he had courageous warriors, no one doubted that fact, there were few modern rifles in his armory boasting only a handful of muskets and blunderbusses, weapons as outdated and inadequate in the modern battlefield as their assegai and shields.

And then there were the Boers. Lobengula feared these hardy Afrikaners more than the British, for the British at least feigned respect for the African while the Boer both *de jure* and *de facto* were anathema to blacks. In 1837 Hendrick Potgieter heavily defeated Mzilikazi with modern rifles, causing the Matabele to flee north away from Boer and Zulu harassment, initiating a tribal mythology of fear for the Afrikaner farmers. While the Boers were outright enemies, the British could not be trusted. Lobengula knew how they had reneged several times in land transfers leaving large black populations under Boer control. And just when matters of alliance and treaty could not get even more complicated, Lobengula heard about the Battle of Majuba Hill where a Boer force had trounced the British soldiers, inflicting 280 casualties out of the 400 redcoats while suffering only two Boer dead. Lobengula had to choose between the British who were often unscrupulous but at least made a charade of respect for the blacks, or the Boers who loathed the blacks but could potentially defeat the British in battle.

Knowing he could beat neither British nor Boers militarily, Lobengula decided to arm his soldiers with as many modern weapons as he could despite laws forbidding the sale of weapons to Africans. Although defeating the English and Boers was probably unlikely with the few obtainable rifles, Lobengula probably intended to at least regain ascendancy over traditional enemies while deterring or blunting any European or Boer attacks until better political prospects emerged. Every effort was made to earn money to procure weapons, from levying fees on traders, hunters and explorers, to the secret employment of Matabele in the gold and diamond mines of the south. Reverend J. D. Hepburn attests, "Every day numbers of Makalanga, tens, twenties, are passing on their way to the diamond field. They report that the order has gone forth to all indunas of the Matabele army, that they are to buy breech loaders and horses; and the Makalanga are being sent to work for them on the diamond fields"[1] (qtd. in Samkange 73). Of course, outfitting with modern weapons an army of 20,000 warriors steeped in traditions of hand-to-hand combat, traditions themselves inextricably tied to social order, was an ambitious plan. However, with his kingdom threatened on all fronts, Lobengula had little choice but to adopt modern weapons and tactics with all haste.

Firearms were not the only technological opposition facing the King. The Europeans brought a veritable array of sophisticated advancements unknown in Matabeleland, some intended for battle while others, just as insidious, were concocted in the forges and labs of Europe for any number of other applications. As Gann and Duignan point out, all "progress" ultimately contributed to the demise of the Matabele nation:

> The whites held the ideological initiative. They also had the physical means to make their power felt. The technological gap between their society and that of Africa continually widened. The prophylactic use of quinine helped to raise the mosquito barrier, which had shut off the interior. The steam engine was successfully applied to land and water transport and brought about a complete transformation in the logistics of trade and war. The steam locomotive penetrated deep into the continent (192).

Factories stamped out rifles in the thousands, new formulae for better explosives bubbled in laboratories, steam ships ferried goods and troops from Europe, soldiers were drilled in the latest tactics and intimately mated with modern weapons; the Matabele nation was not simply facing a technologically superior army, but equipment and training many centuries more developed. From the innocuous telegraph, to the railroad, to advanced medicine and field hospitals, the Europeans with each passing year exponentially outpaced the Matabele who had yet to make real use of even the simplest wheel.

POWER AND CONFIDENCE OF THE PEOPLE

Although supremely powerful, Lobengula still depended on a degree of consent from his people and they were beginning to tire of the perpetual harassment of white hunters, explorers and concession hunters swarming into Bulawayo. Many Matabele, the crack *Imbezi* regiment and the *matjaha* (young, unmarried warriors) especially, wanted nothing more than to kill every foreigner entering their land. If the Matabele could not kill the whites, they were certainly opposed to any deal-making with them. Knowing that even the death of a single European raised political tumult and often an official investigation from the Cape government, Lobengula wisely restrained his warriors by saying to them sarcastically that he would be "only too pleased to 'give them the road to Kimberley' to try conclusions with the Europeans down south" (qtd. in Gann 78). Lobengula's call for restraint was a challenge indeed in a culture that based itself on pride in military conquest. Notions of diplomacy and tact were not only quite foreign, but deeply despised by majority of his people. It is to his credit as leader, and to the Matabele as loyal subjects, that the impis never once broke the King's sacred command despite the constant chafing of having foreigners in the kingdom.

Clearly diplomacy was Lobengula's only option with weapons serving merely to delay destruction. If he were to play the diplomatic card, who was he to trust? The Matabele were so fearful of English treachery mothers would sometimes ask Reverend Helm up to what age did the English slaughter children, and for his intervention on behalf of them in that eventuality (Mason 123). It is Sir Sidney Shippard, the Deputy Commissioner for the Cape, who sums up the situation in Bulawayo most accurately just a week after the signing of the Rudd Concession: "[Lobengula] is sharp enough and farsighted enough to understand that the English alliance might be his best card if only he could trust the English, but there's the rub. England has a bad name in South Africa for breaking faith with natives" (qtd. in Mason 122). The almost pathetic inevitability was painfully understood by Lobengula in a conversation with the trusted Reverend Helm, "Did you ever see a chameleon catch a fly? The chameleon gets behind the fly and remains motionless for some time, then he advances very slowly and gently, first putting forward one leg and then another. At last, when well within reach, he darts his tongue and the fly disappears. England is the chameleon and I am that fly" (qtd. in Mason 105). Lobengula was caught in a classic bind between quelling the warrior spirit in his people and promoting the olive branch of diplomacy with Europeans, between thousand year old tactics and a Maxim gun, between the inevitabilities of the future and the impossibilities of the present. Lobengula was a tragic figure uniquely aware of his position in the trough of relentless and inevitable change.

Critics have suggested the Matabele ought to have ceded control of Mashonaland to the whites for mining and cheap labor, a gesture that could have got Lobengula out of a bind (Stocker 3). But as Galbraith points out this compromise would have merely forestalled the inevitable conflict between the two powers, because they would not long have tolerated such a powerful force on their doorstep, and in time regardless of the volume of minerals and metals found in Mashonaland, those in Matabeleland would too have been coveted (288). Then there was the Swazi king, Mbandzeni who had lost most of his land by inadvertently granting concessions to Europeans (Pakenham 384). Giving land away was out of the question. The Matabele would never have tolerated giving one square foot to Boer or Briton even if there were some ironclad assurance of long lasting peace.

THE RUDD CONCESSION PLAYERS

At dawn on August 15, 1888 Rhodes' agents slipped out of Kimberley in two wagons headed for Bulawayo on a mission to secure a land and mineral concession from Lobengula that would change southern African history forever. Loaded with presents for the king, £10,000 in gold sovereigns and an official letter bearing the Queen's stamp, Rhodes' idea was to give the impression the party was there on behalf of the Queen. On board were six servants including a black American called George, Charles Dunell Rudd, his son Frank, Frank's friend Denny, Frank Thompson and Rochfort Maguire.

Rochfort Maguire was the least likely of men ever to set foot on a wagon, let alone be part of an expedition to visit a "native" king somewhere in a remote part of Africa. A constant liability in the bush with his numerous bags, bottles of scent, toothbrushes and powder, this "effete snob" and "spoiled child of fortune" must have been quite a caricature on the wild trip to see Lobengula, most especially when upon his arrival in Bulawayo he was forced at spear point to crawl on hands and knees across the dung-covered kraal to meet the king (Thomas 190). Rhodes met Maguire at Merton College, Oxford, before Maguire had been elected to the prestigious All Souls College based on his exemplary exam results. In all of Oxford's history such a feat was unheard of for a man of his age. From an aristocratic background, friendly with the Rothschild's and other notables, the highly educated Maguire was tasked with satisfying London by penning the unassailable legal language of the concession.

As a child, Frank Thompson had seen a Matabele warrior kill his father by forcing a ramrod down his throat. He held a lifelong fear and hatred for the Matabele. A former compound manager for de Beers, Thompson gained the reputation of being a tough frontiersman skilled in handling labor, and most useful to Rhodes on this expedition because he understood African etiquette and could speak Sindabele, a language understood by Lobengula. Thompson came to Bulawayo as interpreter and advisor on African custom.

Charles Dunell Rudd, an experienced and trustworthy colleague of Rhodes, was a principal in the Gold Fields, quite wealthy in his own right, and clearly not taking part in the venture for Rhodes' financial largesse. Strangely Rudd did not seem to know of Rhodes' grand plan of northward conquest: "I am quite aware you cannot act freely with [Rudd]," Rhodes told Shippard, "but in case he lays the ground work the objects are the same as though he does not know our big ideas, he will try and obtain what he desires for our Companies whose trust deeds I shall use for the objects I have in view" (Rotberg 257). Rudd's job was to persuade Lobengula to sign the concession that eventually took his name.

Lobengula, son of Mzilikazi, the Great Elephant, as he was known, came to the throne 1870, the same year the young Cecil Rhodes arrived in the Cape. Rudd's description of the King hardly differs from other eye witnesses: "The king is just what I expected of him, a very fine man, only very fat, but with beautiful skin and well-proportioned. He has a curious face, he is partly worried, partly good-natured and partly cruel; he has a very pleasant smile" (Samkange 71). Accounts describe Lobengula as being a shrewd, clever leader sensitive to his responsibility to rule openly and by some level of popular decree. To prevent the king making secret deals, it was tradition that most meetings were held in the public meeting place, the *enkundhla*. Lobengula's throne and royal kraal combined some trappings of European trade with a traditional Matabele backdrop:

> His place, you must know, is a wagon that somebody gave him. There he used to sit on a block of wood in the middle of a great pole stockade, surrounded by hundreds of sheep and goats. Every yard of ground is covered with dung, layer upon layer and the whole place filthy dirty. When you approach the king you have to squat on your haunches, and remain in that position during the whole of the interview (Samkange 71).

During these meetings the King hardly sat idle. As the Matabele were an oral culture, he was highly skilled at negotiation, actively questioning and cross-questioning visitors and Matabele alike with a voracious intensity. Thompson describes Lobengula's negotiating skills:

> Well, it was a bit nasty when the king was in a bad temper. He used to try to catch you out, and make you contradict yourself. And he was sharp as a needle at his own style of palaver. He remembered everything, and if you did contradict yourself, he was down on you at once (Samkange 72).

With the onslaught of whites pestering him in Bulawayo and traditional enemies arming themselves with modern weapons, it was Lobengula's unenviable task to navigate his people through the narrows of political and social change that were rapidly forcing him into a corner.

The Reverend Charles Daniel Helm remains one of the most poignant figures in the Rudd Concession saga, a man whose devotion to God simultaneously made him the savior and destroyer of the Matabele nation. Helm's signature on any agreement with Lobengula was the unassailable endorsement Rhodes needed for liberals and rivals in the Cape and London. To understand Helm, one must understand the power that is the interpreter's, the neck in an hour glass seeing and defining the meaning of each passing grain and seemingly, with just a pinch, to facilitate, manipulate or halt all progression. It could be said that the ambitions of Rhodes, Britain and Lobengula were welded or torn by one man: the Reverend Charles Helm. Lobengula trusted him implicitly, that much is clear, for Helm would frequently be called in to interpret all manner of documents brought by hunters, prospectors, explorers and messengers from heads of state. However, Helm's position in Matabeleland was not that of royal interpreter. Rather, he was the senior London Missionary Society (LMS) missionary in the area who took his temporal instruction from London, while performing his God-given duty of saving the local population through conversion.

In all the years the LMS spent in Matabeleland, there had yet to be a single convert. Though he never issued an official edict forbidding conversion, Lobengula made clear his disapproval of worshipping the European God. In a land where the ruler could command the immediate death of any of his subjects, the king's displeasure was to be avoided. The lack of converts caused tremendous strain in an already barren and inhospitable Matabele missionary community. One account describes how two missionaries, living just yards from each other, were on such bad terms they would only communicate through letters sent via London. Never able to establish a strong and viable foothold in the vast kingdom, the missionaries were more dependent than ever on London and the Cape.

> Had the missionaries been successful prior to 1890, they might well have been in a better position to oppose settler policies of coercion. . . Their base of operation would not have been down to the settler presence in the country. And, therefore, the success of the missionaries' efforts would not have been dependent on settler power. But as it was, the missionaries received land and money grants from the administration that stipulated conditions upon which money grants could be made . . . many missionaries believed that their cause was tied to the success of colonialism. The missionary effort could only continue and succeed if European presence in the country was assured. Rev. Burbridge wrote: 'The crowning horror of all sickening horrors that would ensue on the white man's exit would be the supremacy of the witchdoctor. Though under direct civilized rule his power is not yet broken, it can never be supreme' (Mutambirwa 76).

When the prevailing Victorian mores of salvation through Christianity, Commerce and Civilization are considered, salvation for the Matabele—that is, success for the missionaries—lay in breaking the existing tribal order.

Some historians and contemporaries have accused Reverend Helm of accepting bribes from the Rhodes' camp to help the magnate overthrow Lobengula's regime, either for outright self-enrichment or to gain access to the many potential converts. For example, it is widely known Helm received a substantial subsidy from Rudd for the maintenance of the mission station. There is no proof of the extent, if any, the subsidy or other monies played in oiling the interpreter's tongue during the lengthy negotiations with Lobengula. Merely accepting donations as a representative of a widely known religious foundation does not constitute foul play, although functioning as interpreter while taking money from one of the parties at the table is at least a gross conflict of interest. There is compelling evidence, however, that Helm was unusually active in helping the Rhodes camp secure the Rudd Concession. The intention might possibly have been to have more access to potential converts, "sacrifice of a few to save the many" justification. "Helm was already predisposed to the order and presumed stability which Rudd and Rhodes would bring to the vineyard in which he and the other missionaries had so gallantly and fruitlessly labored for so long," says Rotberg (263). Thomas describes Thompson's diary entry, "Helm accepted a payment of 200 gold sovereigns and within a fortnight was writing to the LMS directors in London recommending their support for 'a strong company to work the Mashonaland gold fields and keep out the others.' 'Helm is our man. He has worked through thick and thin in our interests' " (qtd. in Thomas 192). Pakenham states that Helm insisted the Rudd Concession be read verbatim to Lobengula, yet did not insist that verbal agreements, which almost exclusively benefited the Matabele, also be included in the document, knowing that such omissions would nullify the verbal claims in London and the Cape (384).

Rhodes was notorious for quoting that every man has his price. Indeed, he used money and the influence it bought to maneuver around problems, cajole when necessary, and otherwise grease the tracks of empire-building. It is unlikely, though, that Helm was simply purchased by Rhodes' emissaries for they sought influence through varied means. Helm probably saw the missions under Lobengula were a spectacular failure, so changing the regime, even at the expense of some lives, would benefit all involved — particularly the heathen Matabele. It was a matter of scale: remove a handful of the leaders, even through nefarious means, so that the greater tribe might benefit from Christian salvation. Whether for money or ideological ambition, Helm still undoubtedly deceived Lobengula and the indunas. He might well have rationalized these fabrications as being religiously justified, yet nevertheless he repeatedly lied while abusing his position as trusted interpreter.

Lotshe was Lobengula's most senior induna, the equivalent of prime minister, who advised the King on matters of state. Before assuming this high position, he had been the leader of a famous Matabele regiment long used to winning battles against enemy tribes of the Zambezi and Mashonaland. Not long before Rhodes' emissaries arrived in Matabeleland, Lotshe witnessed a large part of his regiment annihilated by a Bechuana force armed with modern rifles and horses, both of which the Matabele lacked. For the first time the Matabele faced an African army that if equipped with traditional weapons would have been beaten on the battlefield, but when armed with modern European weapons had been victorious. This almost unprecedented defeat by a smaller force weighed heavily on Lotshe and thus on Lobengula in subsequent deliberations.[2]

Later in negotiations when Rhodes' emissaries suggested compensating the Matabele for mining rights with modern Martini-Henry rifles, Lotshe was the most eager of all the indunas to accept. Rudd and Thompson immediately identified this interest and set about maneuvering their discussions to best capitalize on the battlefield experience and political influence of this induna. Samkange claims Lotshe was bribed with a promise of 300 gold sovereigns for his support in seeing the concession signed, but this claim remains baseless (73). More likely, Lotshe saw salvation for the Matabele behind the sights of modern rifles. His advice to Lobengula, therefore, would almost certainly not have been motivated by personal gain but by genuine concern for the future survival of his people.

Called *marana-make* by the Ngwato, the "Father of Lies" and the "Queen's Deputy Commissioner" by the English, Sir Sidney Shippard was highly influential in the Cape and Downing Street. A long time confidante of Rhodes and a believer in his aspirations, Shippard was also a one time executor of Rhodes' will. Rotberg comments, "no other British official could have been better placed to further the diamond magnate's approach to Ndebeleland" (253). Rhodes said to Shippard, "My whole success in the interior depends on my getting my trust deed right here in order to have the sinews of war for our plan" (qtd. Thomas 187). The "our" is significant. Keeping in mind that Shippard was instrumental to British policy in South Africa, he was lavishly compensated by Rhodes, and on a supposedly neutral mission to advise Lobengula on what to do about concession hunters, his statements to Newton on October 29, 1888, just a single day before the Rudd Concession was signed, can only chill the blood:

> I do not think that I am naturally of a cruel or bloodthirsty disposition, but I must confess that it would offer me sincere and lasting satisfaction if I could see that Matabele Matjaha cut down by our rifles and machine guns like a cornfield by a reaping machine and I would not spare a single one if I could have my way. The cup of their iniquities must surely be full or nearly full now. Never till I saw these wretches did I understand the true mercy and love for humanity contained in the injunction to the Israelites to destroy the Canaanites. I understand it perfectly now (qtd. in Galbraith 68).

The fact that Shippard was bought by Rhodes is troubling enough. That a man with such views on annihilating the Matabele should have been in a principal position of power to determine Britain's policy towards anyone, let alone the Matabele, is incomprehensible.

There were still other players in the Rudd Concession, namely traders, explorers and prospectors looking for their El Dorado in the African veldt. Individuals such as Sam Edwards of Tati, Fairburn and Usher who held custody of the Royal Elephant Seal of Lobengula, and E. A. Maund acting for George Cawston and the Exploiting and Exploring Company, were all constantly pestering Lobengula for one concession or another (Mason 123). Individually the Europeans were little threat to the Rhodes behemoth, for one or two men, even a small company, could never fund extensive mining operations so far into Africa. But by sowing doubt and misinformation these individuals could still cause Rhodes surprising trouble. The time was ripe for the magnate to step in, pay off claimants, and seize Matabeleland's minerals in the name of a single large company.

DAYS BEFORE THE SIGNING

On October 18, 1888, Sir Sidney Shippard arrived in the dusty capital wearing a spotless white uniform replete with sparkling gold braid and an array of medals. Clearly Shippard cut a striking figure with his regalia. Mistakenly thinking the commissioner was on a mission to clarify the settler position on behalf of the Queen, Lobengula treated Shippard with utmost respect even interpreting the apparent discourtesy of not kneeling before him as a sign of Shippard's exalted status. While Shippard walked with Lobengula to the meeting place, the matjaha shouted praises to their King, insults to Shippard. Somehow interpreting these shouts of derision as calls of praise, the supremely arrogant Shippard later commented on how much respect and awe the Matabele held him!

After two days rest, Lobengula and Shippard met to earnestly discuss Lobengula's pressing problem of white concession hunters at his kraal. Appearing to be scrupulously neutral, Shippard urged the King to give a concession to the largest company (conveniently the only such large company belonged to Rhodes). In granting the agreement thus, the King was assured the company would have resources to mine effectively, and more importantly, would have the clout to stop perpetual harassment of other concession hunters. Awarding a concession to a smaller company, Shippard warned, would simply allow current uncertainties to continue. He knew only too well Lobengula's predicament. The commissioner simply stacked reason upon reason in Rhodes' favor while soothing the King's fears of English treachery, an irony considering Shippard's entire mission was to secure the concession for Cecil Rhodes. Hassing goes so far as to claim Shippard pointedly assured Lobengula of innocent British intentions focused on mining and not acquiring land (242).

Lobengula was in a bind. His people did not trust the marana-make, the matjaha were bursting to kill every white man in Matabeleland, the Boers could sweep north at any moment, and even his once cowering African enemies (some virtually his subjects) were growing increasingly restless. Concession hunters still swarmed around Bulawayo daily. Lobengula had little choice but to exercise diplomacy between both the British and his own people to secure for the Matabele some respite for the future. At the same time, he had to somehow procure and arm his army with modern weapons for what was clearly an inevitable conflict.

Within a week of Shippard's departure, the King called a great *indaba*, a large meeting with all the indunas to discuss the merits of the Rudd Concession. According to custom, Lobengula did not attend the indaba presided over by none other than Lotshe. At the meeting Thompson metaphorically described Matabeleland as a dish of milk attracting flies; the metaphor was perceived by Europeans to be the most suitable device for explaining to indigenous people complicated legal, political and industrial concepts. He repeated his promise of modern weapons in exchange for mineral rights, adding a steamboat on the Zambezi to help protect them from their newly armed enemies. The Rhodes camp repeatedly assured the indunas of benevolent intentions. In exchange for gold, a metal useless to a warrior nation, the King would be simultaneously solving several major problems. One after another though, indunas stepped forward to accuse the white emissaries of having bad blood. Repeatedly Thompson, Maguire and Rudd were accused of outright greed for wanting all the gold in Matabeleland, rather than a portion, with the remainder going to other concession hunters. To this accusation Thompson responded, "I was not going to have two bulls in one herd of cows," implying he would not accept competition in the Matabeleland herd (qtd. in Thomas 195).

When the indaba dragged into the second day, tensions rose as frayed nerves weakened. At one point Rudd appears to have crumbled when he told the assembly he would be prepared to share mineral rights with other concession hunters, but Maguire pulled him down by the coat tails and Thompson refused to translate. Rudd later wrote,

> A great deal of course passed at the indaba that I cannot put down, the most noteworthy being that Thompson and I, after they showed weakness, explained fully to them their own position and pointed out how they must be driven out of their country if they did not get friends and arms in to help . . . (qtd. Rotberg 263).

Later in the second day after more arguments, Thompson finally jumped to his feet declaring that he, Rudd and Maguire were about to leave the kraal and return home: "I said, 'Yes, Indunas, your hearts will break when we have gone. And you will remember the three men who offered you *moshoshla* (Martini-Henry rifles) for the gold you despise in your land'" (qtd. in Thomas 195).

The effect was immediate. Lotshe brought Thompson before Lobengula, where Thompson was instructed to repeat to the Lobengula all promises and assurances made to the indunas. Still the King was uncertain. Hours crawled by. More assurances. Lobengula wanted reassurances that Rhodes had no aggressive intentions. To this Thompson neatly replied, "[He] who gives a man an *assegai* [does not expect] to be attacked by him afterwards" (qtd. in Rotberg 263). He goes on:

> This made an obvious impression on the king, and after pondering it for a few moments he exclaimed, 'Give me the fly-blown paper and I will sign it.' I then said that according to our customs we three brothers should all be present when the document was signed. . . He asked, 'Are you brothers?' I replied, speaking in the usual metaphorical style, 'Yes, there are four of us. The big one (Rhodes) is at home looking after the house, and we three have come to hunt (qtd. in Thomas 195).

When Thompson, Maguire, Rudd, and Helm (who had been interpreting for the past two days) returned to Lobengula, they found the King sitting on a brandy cask in his goat kraal waiting. Lobengula seemed anxious and uncertain. For the next half hour he refused to sign.

According to an account from Helm and Thompson, the following verbal promises were then made to assuage Lobengula:

1. No more than 10 men would dig in his country at any time.
2. They would dig only one hole or in only one place.
3. There would be no digging near towns.
4. The diggers would be considered Lobengula's own subjects.
5. White miners would fight in defense of the kingdom if called upon (Thomas 196).

The King still hesitated. Thompson contemplated trying the clearing-out business again when at last Lobengula said to Helm, *Hellem, tele lappi*— "Helm, give it to me." Thompson testified,

> As he did so Maguire, in a half-drawling, yawning tone of voice, without the ghost of a smile said to me, 'Thompson, this is the epoch of our lives.' . . . I

asked Mr. Helm to certify on the back of the concession that all things had been done in conformity with the customs, laws and usages of the Matabeli [sic] nation in full Council and after full consideration, and that the concession had been fairly and honestly obtained (qtd. in Thomas 196).[3]

With his uncertain "x" Lobengula signed away his kingdom at noon on October 30, 1888.

To be sure Lobengula was given no time to change his mind, Rudd was on his way to Kimberley by four o'clock that afternoon. When he heard of the signing, Rhodes is reported to have jubilantly said, "Our concession is so gigantic, it is like giving a man the whole of Australia' (qtd. in Rotberg 264). Rhodes now had his Suez to the North.

NOTES

1. The Makalanga were a tribe conquered by the Matabele.

2. The Matabele had faced a white force armed with modern weapons when Mzilikazi fought the Boers in 1836, and again when defeated by Hendrick Potgieter in 1837.

3. When Rudd left Bulawayo he took the original concession with him leaving Lobengula with a copy identical to the original but without Helm's endorsement. Later Lobengula would insist the original be brought back to Bulawayo to verify that the copy was identical. According to Mary Stocker, Helm testified the documents were the same. Lobengula then called upon the leader of the white opposition to Rhodes, Moss Cohen, who after being blackmailed by Jameson (the Doctor described the payment as "heavy") ignored the difference of the endorsement (Stocker 17). The author claims Jameson feared the difference in the document being brought to light because the agreement had not been faithfully interpreted to the full council of indunas, and so since the full council was now active the revelation would prove embarrassing for the king and dangerous for the Rhodes camp (Stocker 18).

Chapter Three

Signatories and the End of Kingdom

UNDERSTANDING THE TERMS

There is considerable debate over whether Lobengula knew what he was signing away in October, 1888. Certain, at least, it was impossible for even he to completely understand the true ramifications of each word in the Rudd Concession when placed in the context of the English legal system. To start with, on a cultural level the Matabele were non-literate. Their conception of the significance of the written word versus the spoken would undoubtedly differ from the Rhodes camp. The Matabele considered a spoken promise as sacrosanct and legally binding as any signed agreement in a European courtroom. This difference is not to say Lobengula ascribed little significance to the written word, for he clearly fretted for many months over the signing, indicating concern over the legal implications of the written agreement. However, as Lobengula was not educated in Europe and could hardly even sign his name with an "x," it is hard to believe the chief would have understood the full scope of the language and syntactical structure written into the Rudd Concession by an Oxfordian elected to All Souls.

Lobengula needed an interpreter to "read" the Rudd Concession. This position was filled by the Reverend Charles Helm, a beneficiary of Rhodes largesse, who translated to Lobengula under the watchful eyes of Charles Rudd, Rochfort Maguire and Frank Thompson. If a historian generously assumed the translation to Lobengula by Reverend Helm was verbatim and truly accurate, one would be compelled to ask why the verbal concessions were not written into the agreement? Even the most unsophisticated European would have known verbal agreements carried no legal weight, yet there is no reason to assume Lobengula would have ascribed less legal weight to the verbal concessions. If Helm did truly translate accurately, not simply speak words to the King but explain so he *understood*, why then did he not insist the verbal assurances exclusively benefiting Lobengula be written into the agreement? The reason is clear: Helm and the Rhodes camp knew the verbal concessions prompting the signing would never even be discussed in the Cape and London let alone be legally binding, and would quickly be forgotten once the signature was in hand.

Of course Lobengula never realized the Rudd Concession was a stepping-stone from the Moffat Agreement to Royal Charter, and legally conceded eventual control of both Mashonaland and Matabeleland to Britain. He would never have known the Rudd Concession was the foundation of the eventual Charter Company whose very purpose was to set up and maintain a government, enforce the rule of law, and otherwise introduce European rule to the area. Blake states, "But what did Lobengula and his indunas really understand by it? The question must often recur to any historian of this strange collision between two alien worlds. . . How far could a Matabele Chief and his advisors appreciate what was implied in the documents to which they put their marks—implied, that is to say, in the minds of sophisticated Europeans with whom they were dealing?" (39). Gann states generously, "There is no doubt that the Matabele understood what they were signing; the matter was fully explained to them by the Rev. Charles Daniel Helm, a member of the London Missionary Society, who interpreted for the chief during negotiations, and whose personal integrity was unassailable" (79). He then goes on to say, "The Matabele 'peace party' obviously assumed that the mining could be carried out within the framework of a tribal economy. . . But in assessing the situation, the Matabele may to some extent have been misinformed by Rhodes's emissaries" (79). Certainly Lobengula knew to an extent what he was signing or he would not have vacillated for months. He knew of course he was making some concessions to Rhodes. That said, unless one is to believe that after three months of wrangling over the agreement, followed by repeated assurances of Rhodes' benign intentions, Lobengula simply capitulated and signed an agreement removing him from power and consigning his people to European rule, he did *not* fully understand the scope of the Rudd Concession and the white emissaries knew it.

The Rhodes camp probably did not originally intend to secure the agreement with verbal promises on the side. As the negotiations became increasingly protracted and heated (the trio had already been in Bulawayo for months, far longer than anyone anticipated), they simply sweetened the agreement with the promises. However, this changes nothing about the clear duplicity and deception in how the signature was obtained.

JUSTIFICATION FOR THE ENTERPRISE

Predictably, Rhodes' emissaries took pains to justify the Rudd Concession to other concession hunters and liberals in London. Two tacks were followed: the Mashona were better off without the Matabele, and being so despicable in European eyes, the Matabele deserved their own destruction.

> Shippard quotes with approval Selous' opinion that: 'the industrious and perse-cuted Mashonas would welcome with delight the advent of British protectors, under whom they would cheerfully labour to develop the untold mineral wealth of their magnificent and healthy country, only too happy to know that their own lives and the products of their hard toil would be secure and above all that their wives and little ones would no longer be liable at any moment to be either slaughtered or tortured or driven into hopeless slavery' (qtd. in Mason 125).

True, the Matabele were ferocious in battle. But also true a great many peo-ple supposedly under the rule of Lobengula had never even heard of them, or at worst, suffered rarely at their hands. For the Rhodes camp and British gov-ernment to broadly claim the Mashona would be better off without Matabele rule, is true insofar as most people are happier when not dominated. The claim, though, could hardly apply to *all* Mashona, and as happy as even the most persecuted Mashona would be at the downfall of the Matabele, it is hardly likely they would choose new domination by the Rhodes' regime over quasi self-rule.

Being so "depraved" as the British saw them, perhaps the Matabele de-served their own fate? True the impis were bloodthirsty. They destroyed en-tire villages to a man. For the offenses of a single person, harsh punish-ments were inflicted on many dozens in the village to serve as an example. Indeed the Matabele reputation on the battlefield was known world-wide even at that time for good reason. To be generous, many indigenous cus-toms were misunderstood such as the disemboweling of the dead after a bat-tle, acts attributed to wanton savagery. At Isandhlwana the British were hor-rified to see their slain redcoats sliced open through the abdomen in a seemingly barbarous assault on the dead. In fact, this cutting was a Zulu custom to free the soul of the deceased and thus an act of respect and mercy for the dead to prevent the soul from suffering further. Since the Matabele originated from the Zulu tribe, their customs were similar. In situations like this, a degree of latitude is warranted for cultural misinterpretations and certainly some "atrocities" had reasonable explanations.

Not that Matabele violence should be simply excused as cultural excesses, because indeed the warriors were brutal, but viewing traditional African cus-tom and warfare through a Western lens presents only one perspective, at best a loaded and culturally charged evaluation. Was battle on the Somme or D-Day less bloody and vicious than conflict waged with spears and clubs? Rather than deciding whether the British held the moral imperative to destroy the Matabele because they were bloodier than the whites, a closer examination of motivations reveals that efforts to overthrow Lobengula had little to do with philanthropy and everything to do with removing an obstacle from the political landscape, especially when fed into Rhodes' lively propaganda machine. Just two days after the signing of the Rudd Concession, on November 2, 1888 John Moffat wrote:

> 'As a military power it would be a blessing to the world when they are broken up. When I say this, do not mistake me. I would not do anything to bring about such a result or to break such faith as there may be between us and them, but I am sure that their days are numbered.' (qtd. in Mason 125).

For Rhodes and the British to secure the Rudd Concession and immediately overthrow Lobengula, imperialistic ambitions were insufficient validation. Such a task inevitably includes the deaths and misery of a great many people, possibly the annihilation of a culture, certainly the destruction of an order. Morality and virtue must function as a spear point, the hard tip of the enterprise to pierce common hesitation and uncertainty. Collective moral virtue is a phenomenal galvanizing force, ironically the precipitant of most conflict. Rhodes could not simply organize the Rudd Concession, be awarded the Royal Charter and then take over a large part of Southern Africa for his commercial interests. That would be self-serving. However, Rhodes *should* overthrow a bloodthirsty tyrant to save the Mashona. Propaganda, therefore, provided a moral imperative to obscure these imperialistic ambitions.

WHAT DID RHODES AND LOBENGULA GET OUT OF THE AGREEMENT?

Strangely enough, a detail in the Rudd Concession gave Lobengula title to a much larger swath of territory than he actually controlled. This curious anomaly simultaneously helped both him and the Rhodes camp. Although the Matabele had been the formidable power in the region since their arrival fifty years prior, much of their empire including large parts of Mashonaland was only a loose suzerainty, whereas other portions had barely even heard of the kingdom at Bulawayo. Naturally the British were eager to recognize this broader claim because they too wanted as much land specified in the agreement as possible. Unfortunately for the Matabele, Rhodes also used this same argument to secure in one agreement his mining claims over a much wider territory than the Matabele actually controlled, thus saving himself the substantial cost, uncertainty and time of obtaining individual agreements from a whole series of other lesser rulers.

In his eyes, Lobengula did not cede any land in the agreement. He simply gave mineral rights to a handful of miners who would come into his country at his pleasure to dig at a single site, away from his towns, and with the understanding that while in his domain they functioned as his subjects. In return for these rights, he received 1,000 Martini-Henry rifles and ammunition, sophisticated weapons when used by a properly trained soldier. He also received 100 Pounds Sterling a month with which he intended to buy additional weapons. In this way he thought he had traded useless gold for modern weapons, money to buy additional arms, and peace from pestering claims seekers. Moreover, he hoped to gain some security from the Boers with a British alliance. After all, he had seen the Zulu annihilated when they opposed the British, while the Swazis had been allowed to peacefully co-exist after signing an agreement. British support could be seen as neutralizing settler incursions by ameliorating the perpetual threat from multiple governments and prospecting companies. The agreement simultaneously reinforced Lobengula's own position within Bulawayo against the anti-concession faction of indunas, because the white miners would inevitably support Lobengula against all dissenting Matabele (Stocker 3).

Rhodes effectively got Lobengula's entire kingdom, every last square inch of land from the tops of the trees to as far down as miners could dig because the Rudd Concession not only allowed rights to minerals, but allowed the miners full power to secure the minerals. Moreover, the Rudd Concession was the crucial stepping-stone to a Royal Charter granting him further exclusive monopolistic control over the resources in Lobengula's kingdom. What had the Rudd Concessions cost? "To out-manoeuvre Lobengula had cost Rhodes little, except lies—and the promise of a few hundred pounds of cash and equipment. Far more expensive was the task of out-manoeurvering other Europeans who had designs on Lobengula's country" (Pakenham 385). A few trying months in Bulawayo, some well-placed bribes and payments, careful and determined negotiating, Rhodes seemingly snatched the Matabele kingdom right from under Lobengula. Agreement in hand, he then set about squaring suspicious politicians back in London.

THE AFTERMATH

After Rudd galloped away from Bulawayo, leaving Maguire and Thompson to assuage the king, rival concession hunters remained to buzz in Lobengula's ear of how he had been swindled into giving away his land and would now await his demise at the hands of Rhodes and the other English. This perpetual talk, which Rhodes later regretted not silencing with bribes, was just the sort of friction needed to ignite the increasingly skeptical and nervous Lobengula, and agitate further the matjaha and indunas opposed from the outset to any such concession.

Rhodes' immediate concern was to cement the agreement by supplying the promised rifles as soon as possible—before Lobengula could change his mind. The problem was how to supply 1,000 modern rifles to a known aggressor living outside the Colony, directly contravening Boer and British treaties. To assist in the difficult case of persuading Robinson and Lord Knutsford of the benefit of arming a highly competent African army that in all likelihood would one day fight Europeans, again came the Reverend Helm: "The substitution of long-range rifles for the stabbing *assegai*," claimed Helm, "would tend to diminish the loss of life in the Matabele raids and thus prove a distinct gain in the cause of humanity" (qtd. in Thomas 198). Shippard and Rhodes added the Matabele would be unable to set their rifle sights properly, thereby rendering the weapons useless. Shippard had the temerity to add that because the technical abilities of the warriors were so poor, they would undoubtedly not be able to fire on their enemies as effectively, thereby proving themselves less of a threat to their neighbors (Rotberg 265). As preposterous as these arguments were and however implausible they sound, many British officials were merely looking for any reason to substantiate Rhodes' cause.

The Church strenuously objected to arming Lobengula, observing the action would inevitably bring untold bloodshed to Matabele enemies, particularly the Mashona. Denouncing the arming in a well-publicized speech given in Vryburg, the Anglican Bishop of Bloemfontein, the Rt. Rev. Knight-Bruce, declared the Mashona needed full protection from the "the diabolical horrors which mark the path of the Matabele impis" (qtd. in Gann 85). "I consider that giving one firearm to any of the Matabele—and everyone must know that it would be used to assist in the murder of hapless innocents—would be an act which, if not in this world, certainly in the next, a man would be sorry for indeed. Such a piece of devilry and brutality as a consignment of rifles to the Matabele cannot be surpassed" (qtd. in Rotberg 265). The condemnation by the popular Knight-Bruce was an embarrassing setback for Rhodes.

Within several days of the bishop's damning speech, Rhodes told Rudd about meeting Knight-Bruce: "Without telling you a long story I will simply say that I believe he will be our cordial supporter in the future. I am sorry for his . . . speech . . . but he has repented" (qtd. in Rotberg 265). Every man has his price. How Rhodes persuaded Knight-Bruce to completely change his

viewpoint has never been revealed, but the shift in stance from such an emi-
nent churchman was noteworthy and critical. With people in the right places
paid to make the right statements or just to keep quiet, Rhodes gradually fortified his final charge to the Royal Charter.

In November 1888, Rhodes decided to cement his claim by publishing a
bowdlerized version of the Rudd Concession in both the *Cape Argus* and
Cape Times (he owned both newspapers). Here he made a point to emphasize
Helm's endorsement and the great favor it was held in by the missionaries.
Two days after publication he added, supposedly from Lobengula's instruction, a stern and ominous warning to all new concession hunters that their
presence in Matabeleland was unwelcome. Like a spark to tinder, the articles
ignited Matabele fury over the Rudd Concession, Rhodes and all whites.
Soon after, Thompson was unceremoniously summoned before the King to
explain these articles. Naturally, Thompson denied anything stating Lobengula had given away his kingdom, but the other concession hunters including
Maund (of the aptly named Bechuanaland Exploring and Exploiting Company), confirmed what Lobengula and so many Matabele feared: the
chameleon carefully took one step closer to the fly.

What happened next is an extraordinarily complicated and bizarre drama
of world travel, deception, and skillful time manipulation that if not entirely
true would be too fanciful to invent. Because a seed of uncertainty and suspicion was planted, possibly by the competing Maund, Lobengula suddenly
decided to communicate with the Queen directly. He told Thompson he was
sending two indunas with Maund to London to personally present a message
to Queen Victoria. The messages carried by Umjete and Babayane, indunas
known for their exceptional memories, would be divulged to no one but the
Queen herself, ostensibly so Lobengula could finally explain his position
without interference from the Rhodes camp or other concession hunters. To
assist Maund, Renny-Tailyour offered a Natal frontiersman by the name of
Johann Colenbrander as interpreter, thereby cementing his group with Lord
Gifford's camp in unity against Rhodes.

On their way to Cape Town, Colenbrander, Maund and the two indunas
stopped at Kimberley where Maund was invited to meet a now agitated
Rhodes facing the possible dissolution of his whole Cape-to-Cairo plan.
Closely questioned about the content of the indunas' message, Maund gave
no ground to the diamond magnate (he did not know the content anyway).
Rhodes then threatened to telegraph Robinson in Cape Town saying that
Maund was heading to England with two common laborers he found walking
in the bush. The meeting ended caustically.

Once Maund and the indunas arrived in Cape Town, they faced three in-
terrogations organized by Sir Hercules Robinson, all yielding not a word of

the secret message. Meanwhile from Kimberley, Rhodes had been actively telegraphing just about everybody to try to avoid the collapse of his north-ward imperialist venture. Within days however, he somehow managed to forge an alliance with Maund's employer, Lord Gifford. Again, every man has his price. Now everybody was on the same side—except the indunas!

With Maund and Renny-Tailyour now in the Rhodes camp, the problem re-mained what to do with the indunas since they still expected to travel to London for a personal audience with the Queen. Blocking the trip would further destabilize the delicate situation in Bulawayo, so the passage to London com-menced shortly afterward with Rhodes' approval. Naturally everyone, except the indunas, assumed Colenbrander's translation in London would prevent real damage from Lobengula's secrete message. Rhodes' interpreter, the newly allied Mr. Colenbrander, would simply filter out any troublesome or in-criminating bits and pieces of information to provide the Queen and the in-dunas alike a neat and tidy account of the situation in Matabeleland. Unbe-knownst to the Rhodes camp, as the *Moor* sailed out of Cape Town on February 6, 1889 there was another passenger on board who would soon prove highly inconvenient to the scheme: the famed hunter, and highly fluent, Frederick Courtney Selous.

Back in Bulawayo the mood intensified. Many scholars believe Matabele opposition to the Rudd Concession was so great that Lobengula's own po-sition was in jeopardy. To aggravate the situation, Maguire caused grave of-fense one day by bathing in the sacred fountain at Bulawayo, then brushing his teeth in the water with a foaming paste that colored the fountain scarlet. The unfortunate Maguire was dragged naked before the King by enraged warriors eager for his immediate execution despite Maguire's pleas of ig-norance. Unfortunately for him, the next day Lobengula's mother died pro-viding a clear indication of Maguire's (and Rhodes') witchcraft. Fortunately for them, Lobengula was not eager to provoke military action from the Cape so he decided against killing such a noteworthy individual. Thus Maguire barely escaped with his life but not without spending a terrifying day await-ing his execution.

Continually disturbed by the buzzing of the rival concession hunters, con-cerned about the legal future of his kingdom outlined in a concession he could not even read, further aggravated by Maguire and the constant pestering of the whites, Lobengula supposedly then retracted the Rudd Concession on January 18, 1899. From Bulawayo came the following signed statement:

Notice:

I hear it is published in the newspapers that I have granted a concession in all my country to Charles Dunell Rudd, Rochford [sic] Maguire, and Francis

Robert Thompson. As there is a great misunderstanding about this, all action in respect to the said concession is hereby suspended, pending an investigation to be made in my country.

(signed) Lobengula

Royal *Kraal*,
Matabeleland
18th January 1889 (qtd. in Mason 129)

Although Rhodes could stop publication of this retraction in South Africa, he could do nothing about the notice having appeared in *The Bechuanaland News* and *Malmani Chronicle*. Regardless of any censoring, it is almost certain the retraction was a forgery anyway because although the original notice was stamped with the King's elephant seal (in the possession of the trader Fairburn), the notice was *only* signed by three concession hunters, Phillips, Reilly and Usher, but had no mark from Lobengula or any authentication from Helm, the only appropriate person in Bulawayo to have legitimized the document. Nevertheless, the tension and intrigue in Bulawayo is made all the more evident by this effort, probably from competing concession hunters, to undermine the agreement. If Lobengula did not specifically retract the Concession on January 18, 1889, he certainly did so in September 1889.

In the meantime there was still the issue of completing the deal made in the agreement. Rhodes was desperate to deliver rifles to Lobengula as soon as possible to assuage the simmering dissension in Bulawayo, the Cape and London, for it was widely believed that if the rifles were not delivered and received by Lobengula the already frail Concession was doomed. With Rudd citing poor health, Rhodes turned to Dr. Leander Starr Jameson, a personal friend, well known doctor and admirer of very tall women, to accompany the rifle shipments to the royal kraal while hopefully using his renowned charm to soothe the agitated King. Because no permits had been received from the Cape to transport the weapons, the first consignment of 500 rifles and 50,000 cartridges were smuggled by wagon to Bechuanaland where they linked up with Jameson and Rutherford Harris for the journey to Bulawayo. The second shipment of rifles and ammunition was scheduled to arrive in February 1890.

To their relief Lobengula was quite taken with the bold, witty and fearless Jameson, and would, to his ultimate undoing, consider the doctor a friend. As Rotberg points out, "Lobengula had gout, Jameson carried a hypodermic needle and morphine, and used both to good effect" (292).[1] Poignantly though, Lobengula refused ownership of even a single rifle, storing them instead in their tin-lined cases at Thompson's camp well away from the royal kraal. He hesitated to take full possession of them fearing this would validate the Concession. Scholars debate when Lobengula accepted the 1,000 guns. Cobbing gives March 1893 as the actual moment of acceptance when the threat of settler incursion from Fort Victoria and Salisbury was inevitable, whereas most other scholars and historians cite early 1889 (77). Lobengula as well as Rhodes knew that receipt of the weapons would validate the Rudd Concession. Knowing this, Rhodes rushed the guns to Bulawayo; Lobengula kept the crates but did not actually open or officially accept them. Cobbing describes how the weapons were stored and maintained by the Company in Bulawayo from early 1889 until March 1893 under the care of certain traders residing in the kraal, but not by the King or any Matabele (78). In this way they could be held in close proximity without actually being accepted.

Was acceptance made palpable by opening the crates and the distribution of these arms to his warriors in 1893, or by the granting of permission to store them within the vicinity of Bulawayo until 1889? By not returning the weapons immediately, Lobengula in fact accepted them. A convincing argument can then be made that in accepting the weapons he was agreeing to the terms of the agreement in full. However, in view of how Rhodes and his emissaries were defining the agreement in their favor and proceeding with little heed to the Matabele objections, it was reasonable for Lobengula to at least keep the weapons until some resolution was achieved. Especially in light of how he saw deceit in European bargaining and understood they would proceed regardless of the terms themselves or how they were struck, and considering how his only defense were these weapons, he could not very well return them and get nothing for the agreement while leaving his people vulnerable to attack. Thus his strategy of leaving them stored away while refuting the agreement is a reasonable measure.

On February 27, 1889 the *Moor* arrived in England carrying Maund, Colenbrander, Selous and the two indunas, Umjete and Babayane. South Africa was fashionable in London that year. The indunas stirred a media frenzy igniting a flurry of bids by high society to engage the Matabele for social events. The two were shown a demonstration of Gatling guns at Aldershot, a naval exercise off Portsmouth and taken to the Bank of England to see for themselves the country's vast wealth (Blake 50). They also met Queen Victoria at Buckingham Palace.

At this meeting Selous presented a very real threat to Rhodes, because Colenbrander could no longer censor the exchanges between the Queen and the indunas. Worse, when it came to prestige and credibility, Selous was something of a hero in England thanks to *A Hunter's Wandering in Africa*, his bestseller published in 1886 followed two years later by Ryder Haggard's *King Solomon's Mines* whose hero, Alan Quartermain, was generally thought to be based on Selous (Thomas 205). As Umjete presented Lobengula's secret message to the Queen, Colenbrander had no choice but to accurately translate the imploring message asking her for help in stopping the horde of white men requesting gold concessions.

> Using language popularized by Rider Haggard and believed to be appropriate for illiterate potentates in far-off lands, the Queen said that she had been pleased to receive the king's messengers. 'They say that Lo Bengula is much troubled by white men who come into his country and ask to dig for gold. . . The Queen wishes Lo Bengula not to grant hastily concessions of land or leave to dig. . . It is not wise to put too much power into the hands of men who come first, and to exclude other deserving men. A king gives a stranger an ox, not his whole herd of cattle, otherwise what would other strangers arriving have to eat?' (qtd. In Rotberg 270).

The letter for Lobengula stating the sovereign's advice not to proceed with the Concession was actually written by Lord Knutsford, the Colonial Secretary, and handed to Maund along with a second troublesome letter from the Aborigines Protection Society. After failing to have the letters dropped into the sea, as he actually tried to have done, Rhodes could only buy himself time by sending Maund and the indunas on the long route back to the Cape—via Rio de Janeiro. With the aid of telegraph and runner, the message could have reached Lobengula by early April. In fact, the letters and weary indunas did not arrive until August 5, 1889.

The moment they arrived in Bulawayo the Matabele response was quick and terrifying, especially for Thompson who had remained in the capital. People came to the Royal Kraal in droves to find out whether the white men had bought the land. He and Lotshe were dragged before a full council of indunas and the King. Squatting in the broiling sun with accusations of treachery and deception being hurled at them, the frightened Thompson soon realized it was nigh time blood was spilled for Matabele pride. As Lotshe, the most senior and trusted induna came out of a hut his sunken face shouted his demise. Accused of having given disastrous advice and misled the king by promoting the trade of weapons for mineral rights, and in so doing been a traitor to the Matabele insofar as Lobengula was concerned, he was sentenced to death. Thompson described Lotshe's fate:

> I saw the poor old fellow stand erect. He handed his snuffbox to a man standing near. He was taken outside the council kraal, and on kneeling down he said, 'Do as you think fit with me. I am the king's chattel.' One blow from the executioner's stick sufficed; one smart blow on the back of the head . . .
>   That night was spent by the Matebili [sic] in putting to death the men, women and Children of Lotjie's [sic] family. It was the most terrible night in

my experience. . . Some three hundred men, women and children were killed
. . . I had just started [for Hope Fountain to see Helm] when I heard a native
following me. . . 'Tomoson,' he called quietly, 'the king says the killing of
yesterday is not over yet' (qtd. in Thomas 212).

That warning was enough. He immediately jumped on the nearest horse and
without a saddle and only an improvised bridle, galloped for his life knowing
once the Matabele smelled blood they were not likely to halt before killing
him as well. Soon he found himself wandering the Kalahari. His horse col-
lapsed, he almost died from dehydration until a passing trader happened upon
him and saved his life. At the nearest telegraph station Thompson cabled his
wife and Rhodes. Rather than congratulate his lieutenant on a miraculous escape, Rhodes threatened him by saying his reward of millions was only
payable upon *completion* of the task at hand. Though terrified, Thompson
bravely obeyed the order to rendezvous with Jameson in Mafeking and return
to Lobengula with Bulawayo seething.

Finally receiving the correspondence from London, Lobengula immediately drafted a response to the Queen's letter. On August 10, 1889, he wrote,
"If the Queen hears that I have given away the whole country it is not so . . .
I thank the Queen for the word which my messengers gave me by mouth, that
the Queen says I am not to let anyone dig for gold in my country except to
dig for me as my servants" (qtd. in Rotberg 271). Conceivably this letter
might have derailed the Royal Charter movement picking up speed in London, but under mysterious circumstances it arrived on November 15, 1889,
taking thirteen weeks when other mail was taking half that time. After months
of squaring and deal-making, Rhodes' Royal Charter was signed on October
29, 1889, seventeen days before Lobengula's letter arrived.

On January 27, 1890 a lavishly dressed envoy arrived in Bulawayo bearing
a curious letter from the Queen. Unlike the previous correspondence urging
caution and impartiality, this letter conveyed a far different message. It was
written three days before the arrival of Lobengula's letter in London, in which
he clearly stated he had not given away his territory.

The Queen has kept in mind the letter sent by Lo Bengula . . . and has now desired Mr. Moffat, whom she trusts . . . to tell him what she has done for him and
what she advises him to do . . . Wherever gold is, or wherever it is reported to
be, it is impossible for him to exclude white men and therefore the wisest and
safest course for him . . . is to agree with one set of people, there will be endless
disputes among the white men and he will have all his time taken up in deciding their quarrels. The Queen therefore approves of the concession made by Lo
Bengula . . . to some white men, . . . who were represented by Messrs Rudd,
Maguire, and Thompson. The Queen has caused enquiry to be made respecting

these persona and is satisfied that they are men who will fulfill their undertakings . . . The Queen thinks Lo Bengula is acting wisely in carrying out this agreement (qtd. in Mason 132).

There is no mention this time of not giving away the whole herd, of giving but one ox so as to be fair to other deserving people. Clearly the machinations in London had reached all levels. Having once seen the Queen as sympathetic to his uneasiness, Lobengula realized Victoria too was in the Rhodes camp. Whether the Queen verbalized support or not, the fact remained the Royal

Table 3.1. A timeline detailing events surrounding the signing of the Rudd Concession. Rhodes moved swiftly and defiantly to first block other European powers from entering Matabeleland, then block other British companies, before seizing the Matabele kingdom for Britain and the British South Africa Company. Money talked and perseverance with good connections Rhodes seized control over territory nearly the size of Australia in only two short two years.

February 11, 1888	Moffat Treaty is signed. Lobengula agreed not to enter into treaties without British consent.
October 30, 1888	Rudd Concession is signed. Foundation for Royal Charter.
January 18, 1889	Lobengula supposedly retracts the Rudd Concession.
February 27, 1889	Babayane and Umjete arrive in London.
March 26, 1889	Queen sends letter urging Lobengula not to give all land to one person.
April 2, 1889	Jameson arrives with first shipment of rifles.
August 5, 1889	Letter from Queen arrives with Babayane and Umjete. Bulawayo erupts in furor.
August 10, 1889	Lobengula sends letter to Queen saying he has not given away land.
September 1889	Lobengula retracts the Rudd Concession.
October 1, 1889 (approx.)	Lobengula's letter retracting the Rudd Concession should have arrived on about this date. It mysteriously takes thirteen weeks to arrive, not seven and a half. The letter almost certainly would have halted the signing of the Royal Charter.
October 29, 1889	Royal Charter is signed. Gave Rhodes exclusive control to minerals in Matabeleland and Mashonaland.
November 18, 1889	Lobengula's letter saying he has not given away land arrives in London.
January 27, 1890	Queen's letter arrives. Victoria only now says Lobengula *should* give land to one person

Charter was signed a full two months earlier, and this reality made Lobengula's very kraal now legally within Rhodes' grasp. The chameleon edged
ever closer to the fly.

Jameson remained Lobengula's guest for eight weeks, bantering jovially
with the King, talking of Europe, and steadily administering morphine to treat
gout pain and induce cravings for a drug only the doctor could supply. To get
miners into Mashonaland, called "settlers" by most, Jameson needed "the
road" approved by Lobengula, a sensitive request with the entire Matabele
nation up in arms against every white. They would have been barely uncon-
tainable should a large body of armed "miners" enter their kingdom. The request put the King in a most difficult position. He certainly feared escalating
tensions within his own kingdom by seeming compliant with white requests,
yet was shrewd enough to know the whites were coming anyway. In this
dilemma the King chose not to choose by abstaining from any decision. Not
surprisingly, Jameson took this non decision to be Lobengula's consent. He
said, "Very well then you acknowledge that you have promised to grant me
the road and unless you refuse now, your promise holds good" (qtd. in Mason 140). To that the King remained silent. Mason states, "So it was done; an
unwilling half-consent from a king who knew that his people were against
him, but who realized better than they the consequences of refusal, who believed Jameson's clear statement that an *impi* would come with or without
consent and fight if need be" (140). Just one year before Lobengula was cor-
nered by Jameson, John Moffat wrote:

> I know very well that nothing is further from the thoughts of either Chiefs or
> people than the introduction into any part of their country of a colonizing pop-
> ulation. However desirable such a result might appear to us, to the natives it
> means only one thing, which they have seen . . . over and over . . . further
> south; it means that the white man having got one foot planted firmly on their
> land will soon have both feet on it . . . till he becomes the owner of all the land
> and the native has become a squatter in sufferance in his own country (qtd. in
> Mason 141).

This John Moffat, who so judiciously sums up the Matabele dilemma, is the
very same individual who vigorously assisted in organizing the signing of the
Rudd Concession in the first place. With this pseudo permission from Lobengula to enter Matabeleland, the Pioneer Column assembled and prepared for
their march.

In 1890 each member of the Pioneer Column was promised fifteen gold
claims and guaranteed a 3,000-acre farm, this land allocation being the first
clear breech of the Rudd Concession. The British Government was silent on
this land grant; Rhodes and the Pioneer Column interpreted this silence as an

unequivocal "yes." An official of the company at the time, Hugh Marshall, wrote, "The fact that Lobengula had granted no land rights, no powers to make laws, nor authority to settle disputes was tacitly disregarded. Preparations were made for allotting farms to those Pioneers who would undertake to occupy them . . . " (qtd. in Mutambirwa 34). "It is highly probable that the British high commissioner at Cape Town knew of Rhodes's promises of land grants to the members of the pioneer column," writes Mutambirwa, "However, the high commissioner did not oppose Rhodes because he was as eager as Rhodes to see Rhodesia under the British and not the Boer, flag" (35). For the 196 men in the Column (only nineteen were genuine prospectors of the type Lobengula expected), Rhodes was careful to choose members with the variety of skills necessary to found a colony, men of able fighting form in sound physical condition and most important of all, a group made up of the sons of as many leading Boer and English families as Johnson could find. The newly appointed leader of the Pioneer Column, the 22-year-old Frank Johnson, who would be personally responsible for the welfare of such noteworthy young men, responded with amazement to Rhodes' request for prestigious family names. Rhodes replied with lively practicality that the column would probably be annihilated by the Matabele, or at least surrounded by them. To their rescue would have to come the British government, duly pressured by families of prominent members of the party! It was all part of the scheme. Aside from their gold claims and farm allocations, for their duty the young men would receive 7s. 6d. a day, six times the pay of a regular in the British army. Despite the danger of Matabele attack and uncertainty ahead, Rhodes and Johnson had no trouble filling the ranks of the Pioneer Column. This was, after all, a grand opportunity for the many young European immigrants to make their fortunes.

Assembling at Kimberley with Rhodes himself there to send them on their way to Mount Hampden (near present day Harare), the Pioneer Column mounted up on May 6, 1890 and rode out into what could likely be a bloody death armed with 117 wagons loaded with rifles, small canons, Gatling guns and a powerful searchlight, both to serve watch for night assaults and scare off any would-be attackers. As Merriman, a member of the Cape Parliament, noted, "There are enormous preparations going on and vast expenditure. Machine guns with sailors to work them. Electric search lights (to frighten the Ndebele)—and all the paraphernalia of modern warfare. I regard the future with dread . . . It is a remarkable instance of the power of one man, for the whole scheme is got up for the glorification of Rhodes" (qtd. in Rotberg 299). Behind the 196 pioneers rode another 500 officers and men of what would become the British South Africa Police followed by a thousand African laborers on foot, the whole column stretching two and a half miles.

Rhodes had worked Lobengula into a corner in his maneuvering of the Pioneer Column. Lobengula rightly feared British reprisal if he set upon them with force. At the same time, he knew the Matabele were at a military advantage if they surprised the pioneers with sheer numbers as they slowly hacked their way through thick bush. If the Pioneers were not attacked while en route to Mount Hampden, they would be sufficiently strong and well suited to defend themselves in Mashonaland from later Matabele assaults. Then again, if the Matabele sought their advantage against the Column while en route, although the impi would hold the element of surprise and hold a larger force, they would still have to contend with a powerful enemy armed with modern rifles, artillery and machine guns, not to mention avenging attacks from the British in the future. As Rutherford Harris put it, ". . . If he attacks us, he is doomed, if he does not, his fangs will be drawn and the pressure of civilization on all his borders will press more and more heavily upon him, and the desired result, the disappearance of the Matabele power, if delayed is yet the more certain" (qtd. in Galbraith 144). Lobengula had little choice but to allow the Column to proceed with the hope more viable options would appear in the future.

Clearly Rhodes still feared northward movements from the Boers who could still potentially ally themselves with the Germans, and at the very least occupy land coveted by Rhodes for both mineral wealth and his Suez to the North scheme. In 1890 some Boers had moved with their cattle from the Transvaal into the eastern portions of Lobengula's territory; the emigration was too far east to factor in the mind of the much-troubled King, now profoundly concerned for the very survival of his nation, yet it kept the threat real. The eastern provinces chosen for the Boer emigration were reportedly secured through a weak agreement with a Shona king, thus giving the Boers some legitimacy in their movement (a further indication of Lobengula's preoccupation, for in the past he would never have tolerated such a slight from a Mashona). With Boers trekking northward into Mashonaland, Kruger then surprisingly intervened and halted the emigration for fear of exacerbating already poor relationships with the British. Nevertheless, the potential Boer factor caused much concern for Rhodes and Loch, to whom Rhodes wrote, "I feel if we do not move in this year [the Boers] will move in front of us so it only shows how necessary the Mashona expedition is, if we intend taking the country before the Boers get it" (qtd. in Rotberg 299). What is noteworthy at this juncture is the weakness Rhodes attributed to his own agreements. Even with a Royal Charter to validate his claim, he understood the potential wealth and political advantage of controlling Matabeleland and Mashonaland were inviting to individual prospectors, mining companies and competing international interests alike. This beckoning to the region underscores not only

Rhodes' problem of fending off rivals, but Lobengula's absolutely hopeless position: if Rhodes was not going to take his territory, someone else would.

The moment word reached Bulawayo that Jameson's "impi," the Pioneer Column, was on the move, the King was under tremendous pressure to unleash his warriors now furious at constant affronts from the whites. Lobengula continued to restrain them, the matjaha in particular, knowing any armed conflict with whites would almost certainly result in their annihilation on the battlefield and sure political reprisals later on. When the Pioneer Column crossed the Shashi River entering Matabeleland, a message was brought from the King asking Jameson why the impi was marching through his territory. Jameson assured the induna carrying the message that the Column was simply a mining work party on its way to Mashonaland via a road prearranged by Lobengula, a working party which just happened to be armed with Maxim guns and artillery. The induna was unconvinced. Johnson responded with a demonstration of the company searchlight, Maxim guns and light field pieces, all weapons new and terrifying for the Matabele who quickly fled at the very moment when an attack would have been advantageous militarily. The Column was most vulnerable to Matabele aggression in what is known as the low-veld, the first two hundred miles of the trek where a road had to be hacked out of the bush for the wagons, men and artillery to pass. At any moment, while crossing one of the many wide sandy rivers or negotiating a *donga* (an eroded wash), the Matabele could spring from their hideouts and surprise the Europeans who could not then easily rely on the firepower of the Maxims and artillery. Still the impis were restrained.

Past the new Fort Victoria, the Column felt safer in the more open terrain far better suited to the scything of the Gatlings and Maxims. The Matabele's chance for attack had passed and the Pioneer Column continued unhindered to Mount Hampden where the flag was raised to the acclaim of a twenty-one gun salute and cheers for the Queen. As Ralph Williams said, "Never, surely, did a shepherd open the door of his fold to the world more foolishly than did Lobengula when granting the Chartered Company's concession" (qtd. in Galbraith 153). Salisbury, the capital of what would become Rhodesia, was founded on September 13, 1890. Here was the legacy of fame for posterity. How many men in history have a country named after them? Rhodes, so newly wealthy, had his own—Rhodesia.

Within days of arriving, the Pioneers disbanded from the new capital fanning out across Mashonaland to stake mining claims and peg their 3,000-acre farms. Thoughts of Ophir, Kimberleys and Witwatersrands were fresh in their minds as the men traversed the new territory searching in every riverbed and donga for signs of gold that scientific reports and boundless speculation assured were there. To a man, the pioneers were grievously disappointed for this

new land was farming country. True, Mashonaland is some of the finest farmland in Africa, but for diamond and gold resources it certainly was not the rich
mineral vein extending from Witwatersrand. In fact, mining was so poor the
only way to extract even the humblest earnings was by digging and sifting a
tremendous volume of earth, a backbreaking task requiring copious labor.
And the Mashonas, despite prior claims they would be eager to work on farms
and mines in their gratitude for salvation from the Matabele (in truth, many
Mashona had never seen a Matabele), were reluctant to work for they were
entirely self-sufficient. The reality was biting: Mashonaland was neither Witwatersrand nor Kimberley—and Mashonaland was certainly no Ophir! The
realization led to a new possibility: if Mashonaland was not, then Matabeleland must be the Promised Land.

Tensions had been brewing for some time near Fort Victoria because the
settlement lay much closer to Bulawayo than Salisbury, and subsequently
came into more frequent contact with Matabele warriors operating without regard to the Rudd Concession now long ago retracted. According to the impis,
white pioneers had no right to be in Matabeleland so why should they respect
boundaries purported by the pioneer population? In practical acknowledge-
ment of the white occupation and with the hope of keeping his army busy and
under control, for much of 1891 Lobengula sent his impis all over the western kingdom on minor raids to keep them away from the settlers. An idle
army is a restless army, and the last thing Lobengula wanted was a group of
idle matjaha rampaging into a pioneer settlement killing everyone. With more
settlers entering the disputed land and with new attention focused on the gold
bearing possibilities of Matabeleland itself, a clash still loomed inevitably.

While Fort Victoria and the entire Matabele boundary simmered, an important legal sequence was taking place in the Cape Colony. The Crown did
not accept the pioneers taking possession of land in Mashonaland, so the
Cape government set about obtaining Lobengula's official consent to allow
the British South Africa Company (B.S.A.C.) legal jurisdiction over the Europeans in the region. In November 1890 Moffat presented Lobengula with a
document changing the legal jurisdiction from that of the King to that of the
B.S.A.C. To this document the King reverted to the Rudd Concession saying
that he had never given such a concession. If he had it was the fault of his induna Lotshe. Enraged by yet another affront, Lobengula angrily drafted a re-
ply to the Governor on January 1, 1891:

Mr. Moffat has asked me to give Mr. Rhodes power to punish those who do
wrong in Mashonaland. They ask for this now but they went into my country
without doing so. Why do they come now and ask? When did we speak on this
matter? Did not the Queen say that I should not give all my herd of cattle to one

man? Have I given all my land to the people now in Mashonaland? Who has got the herd to kill today? (qtd. in Mason 143).

Despite Lobengula's exasperated response to the proposal, three and a half months later on April 13, 1891 the High Commissioner proclaimed the sphere of influence including land to the north and west of the South African Republic, east of German claims, and west of Portuguese territory was now under British control. This British proclamation unilaterally stated that all people entering the territory would be subject to the Company and not the King of the Matabele. The chameleon drew closer to the fly.

Ten days later, on 23 April, the Colonial Office told the Foreign Office that Sir Henry Loch had communicated to Lobengula 'his intention to govern and punish the whites in his [Lobengula's] country' and that there was therefore 'ground for assuming the existence of "sufferance" ' on the part of Lobengula, this giving her majesty jurisdiction in his country within the meaning of the foreign Jurisdiction Act of 1890 (Mason 143).

Soon after, on May 9, 1891, came the Order in Council:

'Whereas', it began, the territories of the Charter are 'under the protection of Her Majesty', and 'whereas . . . Her Majesty has power and jurisdiction in the said territories', the High Commissioner may, 'from time to time, by Proclamation, provide for the administration of justice, the raising of revenue, and generally for the peace, order and good government of all persons within then the limits of their Order . . .' (Mason 144).

On June 10, 1891 the High Commissioner's proclamation was signed in which he "empowered himself to appoint Resident Commissioners, Inspectors of Police, and Magistrates. It was under this proclamation that Dr. Jameson was gazetted Chief Magistrate of Mashonaland on 18 September 1891" (Mason 144). This statement was enacted despite Lobengula's strongest protests to the contrary.

Once Lobengula realized Rhodes' intentions, he attempted to counter and beat him at his own game. Knowing Rhodes would have serious difficulty if there were questions over land ownership, in 1891 Lobengula signed a 100-year land concession with a German financier named E.A. Lippert in the hope that Lippert and Rhodes would fight each other to death, with Lobengula able to stand in the wings and retrench his position (Mutambirwa 35). Lippert soon sold his concession to Rhodes for 30,000 pounds sterling and some stock. Every man yet had his price and Lobengula was again thwarted.

In the meantime Rhodes turned his attention to Matabeleland proper, where it was supposed the gold and diamonds had to be en masse for all the reasons originally speculated about Mashonaland: Ophir, Mauch's "discoveries," and a logical geological conduit from Kimberley to Witwatersrand directly through Matabeleland. Simply put, Lobengula had to be disposed of, the Matabele power broken, and the B.S.A.C. power established once and for all. If minerals and the Cape-to-Cairo rail route north were not enough reason, a final justification for the destruction of the Matabele lay in the immutable fact that a handful of pioneers, spread across Mashonaland could not live in harmony with 20,000 agitated Matabele warriors prowling on their doorstep. The pioneers were not leaving: Matabele power had to be broken.

VICTORIA INCIDENT

In April of 1893 some Shona, under the minor chief Gomalla, cut down 500 yards of telegraph wire on the line between Fort Victoria and Salisbury. When approached by the Company to hand over the thieves, Gomalla refused but finding himself in a bind, agreed to pay 100 head of cattle in fines. The problem for Gomalla was these were Lobengula's cattle because the King owned all livestock in his kingdom. When Lobengula discovered the offense he responded to the Company diplomatically by demanding his cattle be returned, stating that the cattle were not Gomalla's to give and regardless, he was King and would exact his own punishment. Jameson returned the cattle. The incident would have been left as a minute spark had Loch not sent a note to Lobengula underlining how serious was the crime of stealing telegraph wire. In true Matabele fashion, which undoubtedly would have been the King's course with or without communication from Loch, Lobengula sent a force of 2,500 men to punish Gomalla for the insult and to prove his cooperation with Loch.

Ahead of time, on June 26 1893, Lobengula sent an official letter to Captain Lendy, the officer in charge of Fort Victoria, alerting him that his impi was on the move in the vicinity of the Fort to punish Gomalla, but that the warriors were under strict instructions not to harm or harass any whites. On June 27 Colenbrander took two similar letters to Moffat in Bechuanaland and Jameson in Salisbury. Lobengula had carefully warned all white officials of his impi's movements to avoid any surprises or accidents.

True to their orders, the impi harmed none of the settlers in their burning of Gomalla's kraals. Their sweep was so thorough though, they sought and killed every Mashona they could find within the vicinity of Fort Victoria, even going so far as to kill nine Mashona within the streets of Fort Victoria to the shock and terror of the white inhabitants. To compound the problem, the warriors even sought out the servants of the settlers killing them on the spot. Through the streets of Fort Victoria the brazen matjaha marched defiantly, rebuking the settlers but never actually physically harming a single one.

After receiving Lobengula's message, Jameson immediately responded by asking Lobengula to keep his warriors to his side of the boundary, that is, on their side of the *Shashi* and *Umnyaniti* Rivers, a boundary Jameson arbitrarily defined and that Lobengula did not and could not acknowledge. A message was also sent to Captain Lendy telling him to disperse the Matabele impi without getting embroiled in a serious incident, because the British South Africa Company was almost bankrupt from huge expenditures in Mashonaland and could not afford a war. As Jameson put it to him, a war with the Matabele would financially throw the country back "till God knows when" (qtd. in Per Hassing 253). To keep matters even calmer, Loch sent a friendly message to Lobengula assuring him of his altruistic intentions. Jameson cabled the Colonial Office saying that Lobengula's actions were only to punish a band of Mashonas. At that point, the tensions between the Matabele and white settlers seemed dissipated with only details of territorial rights to be discussed.

Then on July 13 Jameson left Salisbury for Fort Victoria where he planned to address the indunas present during the raid on Gomalla and surrounding territories. Somewhere on this trip south, the doctor seems to have changed his mind about how to deal with the Matabele question. Rather than avoid a war that could bankrupt the Company, Jameson's solution was to find a pretext to eliminate the Matabele from power, thereby precluding inevitable problems in the future. Soon after he told Rutherford Harris that he had summoned the indunas to Fort Victoria: "I intend to treat them like dogs and order the whole impi out of the country. Then if they do not go send Lendy out with 50 mounted men to fire into them" (qtd. in Thomas 247). The first Matabele war was about to be fabricated.

Jameson's motives for choosing the Gomalla incident in Fort Victoria to escalate war with the Matabele are not exactly clear. A probable reason for the change in tactics has to do with tensions building between the settlers and the Company over the high rates charged for goods, the problem of labor to work the mines and farms, and the monumental disappointment over failed promises of mining and farming in the new territory. "There were always ample opportunities for grumbling—shortages of supplies and exorbitant prices were a constant grievance. But fundamental to settler unrest was disillusionment. The Promised Land had not fulfilled its promise—there were no fortunes to be made from gold, and the life of the farmer was hard and unrewarding. The Company was naturally blamed for these tribulations . . ." (Galbraith 289). If Mashonaland was not the Promised Land, Matabeleland surely must be. It was a matter of timing then, a matter of waiting for the right moment to amass an army to dethrone Lobengula so the white settlers in Mashonaland could prospect farther south, all while the Company's fortunes would be greatly enhanced by the opportunity. On his trip from Salisbury to Fort Victoria, Jameson must have sensed some factor which made the Goma-lla incident an appropriate watershed moment initiating the eventual timing to overthrow the Matabele—always intended by Rhodes.

At the meeting Jameson and Lendy were seated on two chairs surrounded by fifty armed men waiting for the indunas to arrive. The plan was to insult the indunas and provoke them into conflict. This way the Company could ex-cuse itself from retaliating and then overthrowing Lobengula in self-defense. According to plan, as the indunas arrived Jameson bluntly told them he would only speak to unarmed men. While Jameson and Lendy safely sat with their armed guards, the Matabele contingent reluctantly laid down their weapons and proceeded without protection to the meeting place. Jameson demanded an explanation from Manyewu, the senior induna, why the Mashona had been attacked. The induna resolutely defined how Lobengula had never ceded con-trol of either the Matabele or the Mashona. He was the ruler of the region and the whites had the right to dig for gold only. Near to him stood a fine young aristocratic chief, by the name of Mgandane, of slight yet powerful build wearing a fine head-dress. He firmly but courteously stated to Jameson that Mashonaland was within the Matabele kingdom and thus subject to its laws and suzerainty. Moreover, he pointed out that no Matabele had attacked even a single white settler, with the implication that breaches of agreements and other transgressions were the fault of the whites. Then, quite unexpectedly, when Mgandane was in the middle of his speech, Jameson interrupted telling him to sit down because he only dealt with men, not boys, a deliberate insult to this fiery young warrior who refused to be condescended to in spite of Jameson's barrage. Because he refused to be silenced, Jameson stood up and promptly declared the meeting over.

Jameson issued an ultimatum: The Matabele were told to move past the Tokwe River on their way from Fort Victoria within one hour or they would be shot. The problem for the Matabele was threefold: They did not care to be ordered about by Jameson so soon after defiantly stating their inherent right to Mashonaland. The Matabele also had no concept of an hour (Jameson had actually pointed at a part of the sky where the sun would be in an hour) thus making any move even more complicated. Finally, the logistical problem of moving many warriors was more than could be reasonably expected in such a short time, especially since not all the warriors were neatly gathered in one area. It is a virtual certainty that Jameson knew they could not be past the Tokwe River in the time allotted.

After two hours, with the Europeans just finishing lunch, Captain Lendy was sent into the field with thirty eight mounted men to confront the Matabele. Jameson's instructions to Lendy were: "Ride out in the direction they have gone. . . If you find they are not moving off, drive them, as you heard me tell Manyao [sic] I would, and if they resist and attack you, shoot them" (qtd. in Mason 167). Details of what took place are scarce but the fact remains that the Matabele, in various degrees of withdrawal, were fired upon first by Lendy's mounted soldiers. Even when attacked, evidence indicates the Matabele adhered to their King's specific command and did not fight back. Fifty to sixty Matabele died including Mgandane who appears to have been singled out; his shield, headdress and genitals were taken as trophies (Thomas 249). A witness recounted, "they talked to [Mgandane] in a language he did not understand. He was sitting down when they came up, and they told him to stand up, and they shot him in the pit of the stomach or the heart when he stood up" (qtd. in Keppel-Jones 243). There were no white casualties. Later Lobengula would write to Moffat, "you know very well that the white people have done this thing on purpose. This is not right, my people only came to punish the Amahole [sic] for stealing my cattle and cutting your wires" (qtd. in Per Hassing 255). This manufactured Fort Victoria incident was the beginning of the first Matabele War.

Flushed with his success Jameson decided the time was ripe to strike at Matabeleland and finally depose Lobengula. He cabled a message to Rutherford Harris: "We have the excuse for a row over murdered women and children now and the getting of Matabeleland open would give us a tremendous lift in shares and everything else . . ." (qtd. in Galbraith 298). Jameson continued in the cable saying the volunteers to fight Lobengula could be paid in claims and "loot."[2] With that the Rhodes behemoth turned toward Bulawayo.

The Victoria Agreement was signed on August 14, 1893. For their service each member of the force would receive a 6,000 acre farm, twenty mining claims, five alluvial claims and an equal share of the "loot" (cattle) after the Company took one half.[3] Interestingly none of the eleven clauses in the Victoria Agreement mentioned the Matabele, the first five all discussing land (Mutambirwa 39). To generate the appropriate support at home for the enterprise, propaganda began in earnest beginning with multiple reports of attacks on white settlers and detachments of roving bands of Matabele threatening the whites. On October 2, a company of soldiers on patrol twenty five miles from Fort Victoria was reportedly attacked. Then again on October 5 another band of warriors was said to have fired upon the Bechuanaland Border Police. Although the validity of the reports was dubious, Loch authorized Jameson to proceed with his best judgment.

His decision was to trick the more inexperienced soldiers under his command into thinking that a larger Matabele force was upon them. Taking alarmed reports from these men of Lobengula's impis cresting the horizon bringing with them vast numbers of warriors and imminent death for all whites, Jameson wired Loch convinced him that an overwhelmingly large force would confront them in the vicinity of Fort Victoria, thus necessitating Loch's authorization to use deadly force. Loch responded that if the Matabele withdrew without a fight then they ought to be allowed to do so. If they resisted, then Jameson was authorized to use his discretion to control the situation. With this conveniently vague direction, Jameson replied to Loch that he was now acting on his instructions.

As far as the British government in London was concerned, the Matabele were amassing themselves in preparation for all out war on the handful of highly vulnerable settlers. Now angry, Lobengula wrote to Harris, "I thought you came to dig gold but it seems that you have come not only to dig gold but to rob me of my people and country as well. Remember that you are like a child playing with edged tools" (qtd. in Rotberg 439). In his 1991 work, Pakenham discusses how Loch allowed himself to become the dupe for Rhodes and the Company by receiving what were erroneous and fictitious reports from Jameson in Fort Victoria, then forwarding those reports and his recommendations to London thereby creating the perception of Matabele aggressors. "Loch allowed himself to be persuaded that Lobengula had mobilized his army and was preparing to invade white territory. In fact, the Ndebele army was crippled by smallpox" (Pakenham 493). On July 24 Jameson telegraphed Maund, "You understand the position with the High Commissioner and one must go gently. He is backing us in every way. I cable carefully and the truth occasionally and Capetown does the same. The whole gist is that we must settle the affair ourselves and I mean go the whole hog—as to cables 'all quiet and people at work'" (qtd. in Galbraith 299). Lobengula wrote to Loch, "Every day I hear from you reports which are nothing but lies. What Impi of mine have your people seen and where do they come from? I know nothing of them" (qtd. in Rotberg 439). Lobengula had even sent Umjete to Loch to carry another letter to the Queen, but Loch prevented the passage saying that there was no point in attempting diplomacy when the Matabele army insisted on raiding the Mashona.

On October 8, the Salisbury Column under Major Forbes and the Victoria Column under Major Allan Wilson rolled out toward Bulawayo, thirty six wagons in tow loaded with five Maxim guns, three other machine guns and two seven-pound field pieces, along with a total of 652 whites and just as many black wagon drivers and levies. Loch then decided to launch his own attack on Lobengula by moving a column of imperial troops, 225 Bechuanaland Border Police and close to 2,000 Bechuanans led by Chief Khama himself. "The imperial government, Loch maintained, would have no alternative but to support any actions take by the company against the Ndebele, for 'the natives would never understand that the English might be fired on and attacked on one side of a river while the English on the other side quietly looked on'" (qtd. in Galbraith 303). To his horror, Lobengula now found himself under attack from two fronts with Bulawayo the finish line for two racing armies.

Facing certain defeat, the besieged King made one last bid for peace. He sent his royal brother, Ingubogubo, the trader Dawson and two indunas with a message for Loch in Cape Town saying the Matabele were not preparing for war and had not attacked the settlers. As Dawson neared Tati on October 18, he was surprised to find the area occupied by Goold-Adams in charge of the British forces since Tati was in Lobengula's territory. Instead of reporting that he was accompanied by two *senior* indunas and the King's royal brother on a highly important mission for Lobengula, Dawson foolishly left the Matabele in the charge of an N.C.O. and went off for dinner. Thinking the three men were mere escorts for Dawson, the N.C.O. took the precaution of placing them under arrest. Naturally the senior Matabele on an official mission were shocked at the N.C.O.s order and suspected a trap. As a handful of soldiers approached to make the arrest, one of the indunas started to vociferate and wildly gesticulate in protest. As Trooper Knox, "half turned and told him to be quiet, putting out his left hand to induce him to be seated . . . the induna snatched the sword bayonet out of the scabbard hanging at Knox's side and plunged it . . . into Griffiths' breast" (Clement 82). Two indunas immediately bolted for the horses sensing their only chance to escape. Trooper Knox fired his rifle at one fleeing induna, shooting him through the heart from behind. Trooper Arthur Hume quickly closed in on the other fleeing induna and brought him to his knees with a sharp blow of the rifle butt between the shoulders. Hume reported:

> Whilst he was in this position, I was surprised to see Griffiths, whom I had thought dead, tearing up to us. He was foaming at the mouth and almost crying with rage. Before I could stop him he struck No. 2 induna twice on the head with the butt of his rifle. The second blow broke the stock of the rifle and inflicted a terrible gash on the native's skull: the native sank to the ground, presumably dead (qtd. in Clement 83).

Lobengula's elderly royal brother, Ingubogubo was so startled by the turn of events he remained frozen in place. He submitted to being bound. Lobengula's mission of peace came to an abrupt end.

An inquiry conducted after the suspicious incident concluded that the violent deaths of Lobengula's envoys were not the result of foul play, but of a series of events partially the fault of the indunas and partially of the Police. Ultimately, the inquiry concluded, no steps would be taken against those involved. The final statement on the matter must go to the Reverend Helm: "How can one look the Matabele in the face again. We have for years been talking to them about their cruelty in warfare and killing people without cause. And here for the first time they come in contact with the English under the Command of an English Officer of standing all our talk is belied" (qtd. in Per Hassing 257). Indeed, for Lobengula it must have seemed every event would be twisted for war, conquest and his inevitable destruction.

Soon after the killing of his indunas in Tati, Lobengula finally unpacked the rifles from the long ago-signed Rudd Concession and prepared for war in late October, 1893. He emerged from his kraal daubed in war paint to rouse his warriors. In front of his regiments arrayed in full attire, he raised his assegai in a symbolic pose and thrust it deep into the earth, the traditional declaration of war. In the cathartic dancing and revelry that followed, not many noticed that the shaft of the assegai had snapped—a dreadful omen. The era of Matabele dominance was about to expire.

FIRST MATABELE WAR

Early in the morning of October 23, 1893, an explosion thundered across Matabeleland. Startled troops scuttled out of their tents to see an immense cloud of smoke mushrooming from the direction of Bulawayo only a few miles over the horizon. Returning scouts reported Lobengula's capital razed, the King fled north and not a single Matabele in the capital. On October 23, 1893, Captain Borrow with just twenty men marched into the massive kraal at Bulawayo.

Not a shot was fired on the day the troopers entered Bulawayo. A wasteland of ashes greeted the soldiers as they cautiously walked through the now deserted and eerily quiet Bulawayo. The Matabele had vanished. The city was almost completely deserted. All of a sudden, in what must have been a suspiciously surreal moment, a scene more befitting pals in a London pub than the charred gravestone of the Matabele nation, sitting on the roof of their unburned store were the traders Fairburn and Usher casually playing a hand of poker. Lobengula had given his word these two men were to remain unharmed.

It had been just three days since the annihilation of the Matabele impi on the Shangani River, two since the Battle of Bembesi, sometimes called *Ego-*

dade. At the Battle of Shangani, also known as *Bonko*, the menacing Maxim machine gun scythed into action for the first time in battle with appalling consequences for the warriors whose style of warfare naturally required them to clamber within spear's reach of their enemy. Their enemy, on the other hand, sandbagged, protected, hundreds of yards from even the closest warrior, fired 400-600 rounds per minute in what must have been for the Matabele an impenetrable wall of bone-splintering lead, heaving the regiments backward or crushing them in their tracks. As the popular and prolific conservative English writer Hilaire Belloc versed so poignantly, "Whatever happens we have got / The Maxim Gun, and they have not" (qtd. in Rotberg 441). Not all Matabele were armed with spears and clubs at Shangani. Some were seen fumbling with the unfamiliar shot pouches, gun sights and the awkward bolt actions of the Rudd Concession Martini-Henrys, the identical rifles being raised and fired by the volunteers at them. In cruel irony the very rifles purported to bring the Matabele ranks to technological equilibrium with their European aggressors, now served a dual disservice by inducing the ranks to abandon traditional and familiar tactics in favor of modern weapons fired too haphazardly, infrequently and inaccurately to be of substantial use. If the Matabele had charged *en masse,* as they had been doing effectively since the days of Shaka, rather than holding some troops back to attack with rifle fire, they might have overwhelmed Jameson's troops by sheer weight of numbers. Yet on the other hand, at Shangani 5,000 Matabele swarmed around a few hundred volunteers who proceeded to savagely cut down the warriors with withering rifle, machine gun and artillery fire. 500 Matabele were killed. The volunteers suffered no casualties. Any victory achieved by Lobengula at Shangani or Bembesi against such fortified and bristling positions would have at best been Pyrrhic.

At the Battle of Bembesi, Jameson's troops were again attacked by a large and even more determined Matabele force including the finest warriors in the Matabele army, the famed *Ingubu* and *Imbezu* regiments. Of the seven hundred men in the King's royal Imbezu regiment, there were 500 casualties. Altogether at Bembesi, the Matabele suffered 3,000 losses.[4] White casualties were four dead, five injured. The Matabele still attacked using the formation of the buffalo horn developed by Shaka some sixty years prior where warriors would advance in the horns of the buffalo formation. They soon found that this method of assault was quickly broken up with modern weaponry. Within two days the backbone of the Matabele army was defeated.

"It was a nasty ten minutes," declared Bishop Knight-Bruce in describing the Battle of Bembesi, "especially as the Matabele shooting with the rifles was much better than it had been, and they came on with wonderful courage to within eighty yards of the wagons. . . It all made one realize what those

terrible machine guns mean. It must have required extraordinary courage to
have come up the hill against the fire" (qtd. in Rotberg 442). "Whites had
demonstrated an unquestionable technological superiority that compensated
for their tiny numbers," writes Rotberg, "Withering, repeated firing—a Ndebele prisoner compared it to a hailstorm—had decisively destroyed the
Ndebele resistance" (442). The courage of the Matabele regiments won praise
by all sides who recognized an uncommon determination and loyalty to fight
in the face of such overwhelming firepower. Two of the regiments were dec-
imated almost to the last man. The Rhodesian folk singer John Edmond captured the futility of the Matabele struggle in his patriotic song, "The Battle of
Bembezi[sic]":

> We formed a laager on a hill at midday for to rest
> We saw Insukumeni regiment
> Towards the West
> We swung the seven pounder 'round
> And let a big one fly
> And from the East the Amavene
> Gave their battle cry . . .
> The wild Ingubo with the fierce
> Imbesu[sic] on their right
> Came charging from the Northern Bush
> They were a fearful sight
> And near six thousand warriors
> We stopped them on the run
> The bravest of the brave
> Could never match the Maxim gun.[5]

Indeed on that day at Bembesi, as had been the case at Shangani the day before, the bravest of the brave were cut down in their thousands by superior
weapons shooting from entrenched positions against an enemy grouped for
maximum decimation. In just minutes of active battle, the bulk of the Matabele army had been cut to pieces leaving only masses of dead and fleeing
remnants of a once omnipotent kingdom.

While these battles raged in Rhodes' territory over potential new diamond
and gold mines for de Beers, and over new pastures for the Missionaries,
Lobengula fled north away from his razed capital. Major Forbes and a column of soldiers were soon dispatched to hunt him down. Just seventeen days
had passed since Jameson's troops had first left Fort Victoria until the time
Lobengula burned his capital. After his first bid for peace ended with two senior indunas being killed near Tati, Lobengula met with equally bizarre and
disastrous results on his second and final bid to hold on to some power.

Fleeing from the ashes of his capital, Lobengula was under no illusions over his fragile future and the profound changes already unseating the Matabele hegemony. His only option, weak as it may have been, was to make a final offer of reconciliation in the hope that now the whites had most of Matabeleland, they would be content to strike some sort of bargain with him. In a final irony, all the gold stipulated in the Rudd Concession, an estimated 1,000 pounds sterling, was entrusted to an induna with instructions to give the money to Rhodes' emissaries as a bribe for peace with the message, " 'Tell them they have beaten my regiments,' the beleaguered King said, 'killed my people, burnt my kraals, and captured my cattle, and I want peace' " (Thomas 257). Traveling south, the induna entrusted with the task of brokering peace gave the message and gold to two Matabele who, confused and frightened, circled behind Forbes' main column rather than approaching it from the front where they would likely have met Forbes himself. Behind the column, the Matabele found two straggling members of the Bechuanaland Police. They were given the gold and message of peace with the understanding it would be passed to the appropriate authority in the area, in this case Major Forbes. Instead, taking the horde, Troopers Wilson and David hid their windfall and said nothing of the message to anyone. Had the letter and gold been conveyed it is conceivable, although unlikely, Lobengula would have bought more than a small delay to his inevitable demise. A year later the troopers were found out when one of them boasted of the swindle. The men were charged by a British court, tried and sentenced to fourteen years in prison only to have the sentences quashed on technicalities. As Robert Blake summed up, "History is not, however, a court of law, and there is little doubt of their guilt" (108). Twice in a month, Lobengula's diplomatic efforts were thwarted by either shocking incompetence or outright theft.

On November 4,1893, reports reached Bulawayo that Lobengula was dead. Most authors believe the King, abandoned by most of his people, took poison and was buried in a cave with the opening sealed with rocks. Some authors claim Lobengula died of smallpox. Either way the King was dead and his people could no longer look to their sovereign for leadership and guidance. Reverend Helm wrote, "As you know it is my opinion that we shall never do much good in Matabeleland until the Matabele's have had a lesson. And their treatment of the Mashona and other tribes deserve punishment. But I wish we entered on a war with clean hands" (qtd. in Galbraith 307). "The whole matter of this Matabele war has been so unrighteous that a searching inquiry should be made," he adds (qtd. in Thomas 260). This very same Reverend Helm had been the principal interpreter to Lobengula of the Rudd Concession and the principal reason he was tricked into signing it. Although he speaks of "clean hands" it was his signature alone that gave the Rudd Concession unassailable authenticity in the Cape and London. "[Lobengula] was a gentleman in his way," wrote John Moffat, "and was foully sinned against by Jameson and his gang" (qtd. in Thomas 260). The clergyman Moffat, trusted by Lobengula as Moffat's father was loved and trusted by Mzilikazi, also played a pivotal role in convincing the King to sign the Rudd Concession. The embattled Matabele rarely trusted the businessmen, sometimes the traders, but often the missionaries. Compelling evidence shows that almost to a man even the Matabele sympathizers and clergy had their price and were complicit in eventually cheating the sovereign.

On July 18, 1894 the Chartered Company's jurisdiction over Matabeleland was confirmed: The Matabele kingdom ceased to exist. They say the wheels of justice turn slowly and they turned too late to save the Matabele, but they did on 26 March, 1902 when Rhodes too died an untimely death from the heart attack he feared for so long. "So little done, so much to do," he is said to have uttered as he passed. He had prepared a princely monument for himself in Cape Town with grand crouched bronze lions and a horse called "Energy" poised to leap into the hinterland—but his body was interred in World's View at the Matopos, a sacred place for the Matabele near Bulawayo. Mzilikazi is buried just fifteen kilometers away. Lobengula's grave was only officially discovered and examined in 1946. Their names are rarely mentioned today whereas Rhodes is known worldwide. Covered with a granite slab and bronze plate inscribed with the words, "Here Lie the Remains of Cecil John Rhodes." It looks out over what is left of the Matabele kingdom, toward Bulawayo which still strongly resembles the colonial city of Rhodes' making, then over the country that despite changing its name from Rhodesia to Zimbabwe remains torn between the imprint of colonialism and renewed recognition of black cultural heritage.

What was written in this agreement to compel Lobengula to sign and Rhodes to push so forcefully for a "legal" recognition of his claims? How has this one document come to define this period and set about rifts and land disputes still raging in the country today?

NOTES

1. Lobengula's gout was probably caused by the consumption of copious quantities of red meat and champagne, the latter a favorite gift of concession hunters.

2. According to Pakenham, the title for Mashonaland was based on legal agreements whereas the title for Matabeleland was based on conquest, and in the European

ideals of conquest all that belonged to the defeated king now belonged to the Company (495).

3. The eventual seizing of cattle from the Matabele brought tragic and unforeseen unraveling of the Matabele culture. Cattle were central to Matabele life. Although technically the king owned almost all the cattle, no one was brave enough to claim ownership to more than 100 head. The vast herds were tended by the Matabele who all enjoyed the milk from the cattle and the prestige of quasi-ownership. In 1895 the Company decided that of the 200,000 head so far confiscated none would be returned to the Matabele, and a further 33,000 of the remaining 74,000 head would also be seized for distribution as loot to settlers and other Europeans (Pakenham 496). After the decimating of the herds by the Company, the Matabele were then left with an estimated 41,000 head of the original 300,000 cattle.

4. Casualty figures are a curious microcosm of political warfare. It is almost assumed these figures are contorted on both ends, by politicians for the home front and in the field by field soldiers gilding their heroism. In the context of colonial history this tendency to exaggerate is exacerbated because the Matabele were illiterate leaving only the victors to make the claims now written to history, while the Matabele's oral tradition slowly faded. Strikingly, a curious source of rhetorical plausibility underlies battles of the Matabele War: the surprise witness. Some in Jameson's army were so horrified by the savagery of the machine-gunning, they testified to the press and other pertinent groups about the number killed. Presumably these surprise witnesses would provide more accurate casualty figures while simultaneously still denouncing or at least highlighting the atrocity committed against their enemy. Of course the numbers by this measure remain hopelessly subjective. The sprawling casualty figures and convenient round numbers are suspect. The casualty figures presented in this work are a distillation of numerous claims.

5. *Laager*—An Afrikaans word meaning a defensive wagon enclosure whereby wagons are tied together end-to-end forming a circle or square behind which the defenders store their belongings, cattle and families while firing rifle, canon or machine-gun on their attackers.

Insukumeni—A Matabele regiment made up of Zulu stock.

Seven pounder—Artillery piece.

Amavene—A Matabele regiment stationed near the present day city of KweKwe.

Ingubo—A Matabele regiment comprised mostly of younger warriors.

Chapter Four

An Examination
of the Rudd Concession

A TRANSCRIPT OF THE AGREEMENT

Know all men by these presents that whereas Charles Dunell Rudd of Kimberley Rochfort Maguire of London and Frances Robert Thompson of Kimberley here-inafter called the grantees have covenanted and agreed and do hereby covenant and agree to pay to me my heirs and successors the sum of One hundred Pounds sterling British Currency on the first day of every lunar month and further to de-liver at my Royal Kraal one thousand Martini-Henry Breech-loading Rifles to-gether with one hundred thousand rounds of suitable ball cartridge five hundred of the said Rifles and fifty thousand of the said cartridge to be ordered from England forthwith and delivered with reasonable dispatch and the remainder of the said Rifles and Cartridge to be delivered so soon as the said grantees shall have com-menced to work mining machinery within my territory and further to deliver on the Zambesi river a Steamboat with guns suitable for defensive purposes upon the said river or in lieu of the said Steamboat should I so elect to pay to me the sum of five hundred pounds sterling British Currency upon the execution of these presents I Lobengula king of Matabeleland Mashonaland and certain adjoining territories in the exercise of my Sovereign powers and in the presence and with the consent of my Council of Indunas do hereby grant and assign unto the said grantees their heirs representatives and assigns jointly and severally the complete and exclusive charge over all metals and minerals situated and contained in my kingdoms Principalities and dominions together with full power to do all things that they may deem neces-sary to win and procure the same and to hold collect and enjoy the profits and rev-enue if any derivable from the said metals and minerals subject to the aforesaid payment and whereas I have been much molested of late by divers persons seeking and desiring to obtain grants and concessions of Land and Mineral rights in my territories I do hereby authorize the said grantees their heirs representatives and assigns to take all necessary and lawful steps to exclude from my kingdoms princi-palities and dominions all persons seeking land metals minerals or mining rights

82

therein and I do undertake to render them such needful assistance as they may from time to time require for the exclusion of such persons and to grant no concessions of land or mineral rights from and after this date without their consent and concurrence provided that if at any time the said monthly payment of one hundred pounds shall be in arrear for a period of three months then this grant shall cease and determine from the date of the last made payment and further provided that nothing contained in these presents shall extend to or affect a grant made by me of certain mining rights in a portion of my territory south of the Ramakoban river which grant is commonly known as the Tati Concession.

This given under my hand this thirtieth day of October in the year of our Lord Eighteen hundred and Eighty-Eight at my Royal Kraal.

his

Lobengula X

mark

Witnesses:
(Signed)   (Signed)
Chas. D. Helm   C. D. Rudd
J. G. Dreyer   Rochfort Maguire
F. R. Thompson

REVEREND HELM'S ENDORSEMENT OF THE CONCESSION

(Written on the Left Hand Side of the Rudd Concession)
I hereby certify that the accompanying document has been fully interpreted and explained by me to the Chief Lobengula and his full Council of Indunas and that all the Constitutional usages of the Matabele Nation had been complied with prior to his executing same.

Dated at Umguza River this thirtieth day of October 1888.

DOCUMENT-LEVEL RELEVANCE

The Rudd Concession was pivotal to southern Africa's history.[1] It was not merely an agreement by which Lobengula ceded mineral control to Cecil Rhodes, nor even an agreement in which he effectively signed himself out of power and his people into becoming de facto subjects of the British Empire. It was the crucial keystone of Rhodes' African plan, his endeavor to protect a diamond and gold monopoly while advancing his patriotic passion of promoting the British Empire throughout Africa.

Cecil Rhodes obtained the Concession for one purpose: to secure a Royal Charter. Without it, one can only speculate how else the Charter would have been obtained since it was British policy never to award a monopoly over disputed territories. It was crucial for his plans because it gave him not only exclusive mineral rights and *de facto* political control, but a guarantee the British government would politically and militarily stand behind him and the territory. Especially when reinforced by the Charter, the Concession immediately ensured for Rhodes the protection for his mineral monopoly in the Cape Colony, Pretoria and the Matabele kingdom. With the British flag behind him, he could dismiss harassing prospectors and meddling governments alike. Furthermore, it promoted his ambition of a Cape-to-Cairo railway establishing British trade and colonization throughout Africa, by preventing competing nations from blocking his northward movement. With the Boers and Germans checked and competitors relegated to the sidelines, the Rudd Concession paved the way for British domination of the continent.

Securing the agreement can hardly be described as exclusively the work of Rhodes. From the authorization to ship arms through cloistered back-room agreements establishing the Royal Charter, to the convenient assistance in Bulawayo of prominent British politicians, and even to the assurance of military support for Rhodes, the agreement was proof of paternal support of such ventures from the British and Cape governments. London was interested in promoting trade in Africa for British industry. Politicians and key individuals were also interested in self-advancement, a powerful motivation at this time. Cecil Rhodes provided the opportunity for governments and well-placed individuals alike to realize goals of all kinds that in Europe would have been impossible, and so in this way found active support on all levels for practically anything he wanted to do.

The Church saw every justification for colonizing Matabeleland. Hearkening back to Livingstone's plaintive call from Westminster to heal the "open sore of the world," breaching Bulawayo was a moral and ethical imperative in which proselytizing was an English duty to save the heathen Matabele. Since the abortive missionary work of Moffat and others in the LMS, Matabeleland had seen not one convert in the two decades since missionary stations were established in the area. This was hardly surprising since Lobengula frowned upon conversion, seeing the shift in allegiance from worship of the king to worship of a God to be treasonous and therefore punishable by death. Ruling by fear, the tribal chief was implacably opposed to conversion because he knew that control of the mind was control of the tribe. He was not about to share his power with anyone! Conquering Matabeleland, as the Concession was designed eventually to do, would remove the main obstacle of conversion and icon of heathen impenetrability for the missionaries—Lobengula.

Matabeleland was a crucial but uncertain territory for Britain as well. While Lobengula remained in power he could contravene the Moffat Treaty and sign agreements with the Germans and Portuguese or worse, the Boers. Any such treaty with another nation could block Rhodes and the British from seizing this massive swathe of land right across the heart of central Africa. The Matabele could even be forcibly overrun by the Boers who would then seize the wealth of the region and become rich enough to more defiantly oppose British endeavors in the area. The interests of both Rhodes and the British demanded that despite the potential financial cost of the colonization, Matabeleland must eventually fall into the "right" hands. As far as the British were concerned, though Rhodes was promoting his own mining interests at least he was British. As far as Rhodes was concerned, he was securing his mineral monopoly because he was British.

As the foremost naval power in the world and arguably the dominant European power at the turn of the nineteenth century, it was unlikely the British would allow their nation to stand idle while a substantial kingdom just to the north of the crucial Cape Colony remained un-claimed by Europeans. They had the resources, and more importantly, the national pride to demand of themselves they move boldly into Matabeleland. Rhodes heard their call and maneuvered himself to be well-placed to answer Britain's needs while promoting his personal agenda. This he did by reminding the English of their historical prowess and professed God-given right to rule the world. More significantly, Cecil Rhodes *proved* their right-to-rule by emerging with dizzying force to be Africa's most dominant figure south of the Zambezi. He was their greatest empire builder and his foundational tool to northward expansion of the British Empire was the Concession. For this reason alone the agreement merits language-level analysis to determine what in the prose, arrangement or rhetorical construction led Lobengula to so disastrously sign away his power in 1888.

What in the agreement accomplished so many goals? How could a willingly signed page of hand-written text secure a piece of Empire the size of Australia for Rhodes and consign the Matabele to be subjects of a colonial master on the far side of the world?

PURPOSE OF THE AGREEMENT ACCORDING TO RHODES

The purpose of the agreement according to Cecil Rhodes was simply to secure the Royal Charter. He initiated meetings between his emissaries and Lobengula, funded trips to Bulawayo, paved the political pathways in the Cape and London for the legal foundation the agreement was to provide. The newspapers under his control were ready to manipulate public opinion, and the Church was prepped to provide moral benediction. These were all simple tools that assured he could undertake his grander aspirations in the region free from harassment of competitors and with the backing of the power of the British government.

Without the Concession, Rhodes' future plans for African expansion remained vulnerable. At any moment, vast new mineral sites could be discovered in the north undoing his precious mineral monopoly. Rhodes' monopoly was only intact if no other major mineral sites were discovered. While South Africa held the world's largest diamond and gold mines, who could say more would not be found at any moment, potentially relegating the magnate to insignificance? From the beginning of his days on the diamond diggings at Kimberley, Rhodes defined his business model on his rigid control of diamond output to regulate market prices. All he had worked for and all his success and future plans, could at any moment be undone with a major discovery by any one of the horde of prospectors swarming the region. Rhodes was on top—but only for the time being.

Rhodes' Audience

The agreement was written to persuade a specific, powerful audience in the Cape and London. The importance of this point cannot be overstated. The audience for the agreement was neither Lobengula nor the Matabele, nor any black African for that matter. It was designed to convince the white political and legal leaders to recognize his claim. Although the agreement served also to prove to other concession hunters the Matabele kingdom's mineral wealth belonged exclusively to Rhodes, the Concession was designed to unequivocally assure London that the Matabele government fully consented to these mining enterprises. By proving the territory was *uncontested* by other European powers, concession hunters, and most importantly by Lobengula and his indunas, the British government could then grant the Royal Charter to Rhodes. If the agreement had been vague about the mineral ownership, the exclusivity of the mining enterprise, or Lobengula's approval, the Charter would not have been granted. It was fundamental then to persuade the audience that mattered most: the Europeans.

Why was Lobengula not the primary audience? Of course he was the most important person the agreement was meant to persuade, but the prose style was not written so much with him in mind since it was commonly known he was illiterate. Lobengula's knowledge was shaped not by the agreement but by how it was interpreted to him. Rhodes and his camp knew, however, that Europeans would pore over every word of the legalese, and thus it was critical they be assured not only was the agreement binding, but that it was freely signed and gave Rhodes a monopolistic scope.

Lobengula's Purposes

Lobengula had a very different purpose for the Concession. He intended it to shore up the Matabele position in the rapidly shifting political milieu of 1888 Africa. Pressured from all fronts, including from internal factions, he was desperate to strengthen himself in the face of potential Boer and British invasion and perpetual harassment from the horde of European concession hunters in Bulawayo. Existing Matabele supremacy was over. He recognized this even if many of his subjects and indunas did not. To avert their almost inevitable destruction from a multitude of threats, he had to act immediately.

He imagined his solution was modern firearms. Armed with knobkerries and assegais, his impis crushed their traditional enemies with a ferocity known world wide. Yet, the bravery of impis armed with such primitive weapons was futile when confronted with modern rifles and machine guns firing 400-600 rounds per minute. Unless he could re-arm them with somewhat comparable modern weapons, the supremacy of the Matabele was doomed. What Lobengula failed to realize, however, was that these weapons would not be of much use without training and drilled expertise.

He did not see the Rudd Concession as a political agreement. The King knew how agreements signed by other chiefs with the Europeans had been repeatedly broken and how other tribes were quickly ensnared by legalese, clever loopholes, and convenient lapses in interpretation. The Matabele were not seeking declarations of peace and friendship in which the Europeans could maneuver and buy time to better prepare themselves to attack him later. Moreover, declarations of peace and friendship did nothing to resolve the armament problem. Whatever time could be bought with such a peace agreement would only allow Lobengula's enemies to better equip and train themselves, all while his warriors were struggling to compete with primitive weaponry. He realized no political peace agreement would stop Europeans amassing on his borders when gold and diamonds were suspected there. Therefore, the Matabele sought a pragmatic agreement to secure weapons and money to buy more. In his view, quite rightly as time would tell again and again, security, peace and independence in Africa were only achievable at the end of a Martini-Henry barrel.

To achieve so valuable an objective, the British and Rhodes were willing to trade the weapons Lobengula needed so badly. While Rhodes was not the only person willing to trade them for exclusive mineral rights, he was the only contender able to actually secure arms through his business and political connections in England and the Cape. On the other hand, the minerals the whites wanted were of no use whatsoever in the pragmatic culture of Bulawayo. Gold was too soft; diamonds were of no importance. Although Lobengula was keenly aware of the risk, the trade of minerals for guns outlined in the Rudd Concession appeared ideal and seemed to hold the only hope of salvation from the seemingly relentless forces on his borders.

To add urgency, the Matabele hated and feared the Boers. From the days of Mzilikazi two generations earlier when the Matabele had been defeated by Hendrick Potgieter, they were anathema to Bulawayo. This feeling was made more poignant by the Boers' apparent invincibility in battle. After all, it was the Boers who had defeated the mighty British army at Majuba Hill in 1881. If the Boers had marched north in the Great Trek in 1836 and 1844 to escape their influence, who was to say they would not do so again in 1888 or at any other time? And if they did move north again in a second Great Trek, would they would head directly for the Matabele kingdom?

Political chafing aside, the Matabele knew only too well how the Boers coveted the rich farmland in the Matabeleland and Mashonaland so ideal for ranching and agriculture. Moreover, they knew how the Boers were already profiting from Witwatersrand and would inevitably seek further expansion of mineral wealth in their kingdom. In light of the overall attractiveness of the isolated geography and potential wealth in the region, for many in Bulawayo the threat of Boer invasion was perceived as a certainty that had to be repelled at all costs.

Lobengula knew no peace agreement with Europeans would last. Their only deterrent was equal and formidable firepower. While other concession hunters offered promises, Rhodes brought one thousand modern weapons and money to the table. He offered palpable protection on Matabele terms. At best with other agreements Lobengula would get only promises of protection while remaining subservient to control of the Europeans or Boer power. With Rhodes he would get weapons useful even if the whites reneged. It appeared the only solution to the seemingly indomitable array of threats: the agreement bought time and opportunity to arm in an increasingly bleak situation. It was for this reason he could not so easily tear up the Concession when he detected dishonesty: he was caught in a bind with no good options—the essence of the fly and chameleon analogy.

Lobengula's Audience

Surprisingly, Lobengula's audience was quite similar to Rhodes' although their goals of persuasion were antithetical. Whereas Rhodes was looking primarily to persuade the government in London to grant him a Royal Charter based upon the Rudd Concession, Lobengula was looking to extricate his kingdom from a series of predicaments. The Matabele wanted to communicate with the British government a message of cooperation, that their people were friendly to them as opposed to the Boers, Portuguese and Germans. Although the Concession was not a political agreement, it did serve for Lobengula as a *de facto* declaration of good will because the Matabele could just as easily have made overtures to other governments. In return for implied goodwill, the Matabele hoped for British protection because they would then be compelled to protect their own interests in his kingdom. The Boers would in turn fear reprisal from a British army if they intervened. In this way it worked as a declaration to the audience of an implied alliance and shield of protection from the British government.

The intended audience for the Matabele was also the horde of prospectors constantly pestering the King in Bulawayo. By signing one agreement with one large company he hoped other prospectors would back away. If they left Bulawayo voluntarily or by force as the signatories would be bound and willing to ensure, a major source of tension for the Matabele would then be eliminated.

Lobengula intended his own people to be an audience as well. Matabele warriors were becoming harder to restrain in their uneasiness over mounting European pressure and the ever increasing numbers of whites in the country. Many longed to annihilate every European there. Lobengula knew such an outburst would bring savage retribution from a far superior force. He continually restrained his army often at the expense of his own standing as chief. Some of Lobengula's own indunas and a sizeable percentage of his army, notably the Matjaha, had even begun discretely questioning his resolve to meet the threats. Although the same Matabele were outraged, Lobengula entered an agreement with Rhodes. Especially considering the poor record the whites had in keeping to agreements with other tribes, it was hoped at least the rifles and ammunition would pacify his impis. Crates of modern weapons would prove his determination to face the threats with real force.

HOW THE BRITISH INTERPRETED THE CONCESSION

As was the intention of its authors, the Rudd Concession is unmistakably an agreement written by the British for the British. Crafted in their high style, the opening statement of the agreement defines indelibly the tone of the author toward both his subject and audience (Miles, Bertonasco, Karns 207). The author is meticulously thorough, painstaking and deliberate in his careful outline of pertinent details. The tone is respectful but dominating. Far from being written to enlighten, the tone towards the author conveys implacable authority to expound the case of the Rudd Concession to the educated audience. As though from one gentleman to another, it seeks neither to bully nor grovel, only to plead rationally, legally and calmly the case for mineral exploitation in Matabeleland.

The tone and style are ideal for the document's purpose and intended audience. Although ostensibly written by Lobengula, the authors were careful to write the document in the tone and style of a classically educated Englishman. This style conveys the authority and validity one would expect of a gentleman landowner engaging in a legitimate exchange of goods and property. It gently masquerades Lobengula as European gentry, not as an illiterate King in a dusty kraal of Southern Africa. The author cleverly primes the reader with the impression he is educated, sophisticated and astute enough to pass for the king of any European country, thereby precluding questions of understanding, interpretation and legal legitimacy. Naturally the thought of Lobengula actually writing the agreement is absurd. The persona concocted by the tone and style legitimizes the agreement by suggesting the contract was authored and signed by two educated Europeans, each with equal understanding of their own legal conventions.

Of course one look at Lobengula's tremulous signature shows the King could scarcely write his name, let alone author or even conceive such a legal document. Shrewd, insightful, perceptive, Lobengula was a worthy adversary in the arena of African politics. In the forum of an English courtroom, however, the cultural abyss was as great for Lobengula as the nuances and subtleties of his culture would be for any European in Matabeleland. The tone and style of the document supposedly communicating the Matabele King's thoughts and intentions was a rather cunning ruse. By priming the audience to assume Lobengula was a cultural equal, the audience factors out the possibility of cultural dissonance, a condition which would otherwise nullify the agreement almost immediately. After all, Lobengula could hardly write and sign something he did not comprehend. By removing the question, "Does Lobengula even understand what this agreement means?" and replacing it with the assumption of full knowledge, the audience is then allowed to skip past legitimization and jump straight to the legal scope of goods and services defined.

As a basis of comparison, if Lobengula had somehow written the Rudd Concession himself, one can assume it would be saturated with various cultural signifiers, foreign, confusing, and perhaps even completely nonsensical to the barristers and politicians in London. For example, if he wrote it by referencing tenets of ancestral worship and animistic beliefs commonplace in Matabele society at the time and known even by children, followed by metaphorical descriptors defining scope and variance, then concluding with the invocation of cultural mythology for the purpose of authentication, the English audience could probably not easily leap past a stringent evaluation of the legitimacy of the document. Before the scope could be determined, the barristers and politicians would have to decipher what Lobengula was even talking about. The audience in this example would be as immobile, vulnerable, and impotent as Lobengula was when faced with the translator's interpretation of the legalese. In this way tone and style, therefore, function as vehicles to shuttle the contract past the quagmire of a legitimacy evaluation and straight to a consensus of scope.

Just as the tone and style of the agreement present Lobengula as an educated man capable of understanding the subtleties of legalese, the first person prose thrusts upon the King the full onus for the creation of it. Although the audience for the agreement was not present during the drafting or the signing, they presumably realized Lobengula had not written the Concession himself. Subconsciously, however, the repeated references to personal pronoun 'I' unmistakably communicates the context of each sentence as being from Lobengula personally. The true authors not only included the personal pronoun to imply he drafted the document, but the more profound implication is because he drafted the document he must have understood it. If he drafted and understood the document, then he surely must agree with the content!

Buried deep remain the true authors, Rochfort Maguire and Charles Dunell Rudd. They are mentioned by name only once, except when acting as signatories. In all other instances they and Rhodes are referenced by the sterile legal term, "grantees." Although their names are trumpeted on the first line of the Concession, a standard and expected practice for an agreement, the authors and their association with Cecil Rhodes recedes further into the document, ensuring the reference to Rudd and Maguire become only a bland legal point of fact. The purpose behind keeping the names of the grantees hidden for almost the entire document is to throw the weight of responsibility and understanding on Lobengula. If someone were to read the Concession without any knowledge of the events leading up to the signing, it would be fair to assume the grantees played little or no part whatsoever in conceiving the document. The grantees appear almost as a benign backdrop to the genesis of the Concession. The implication is that the document was Lobengula's work entirely, and the grantees merely benefactors of a fruitful business arrangement. The true authors have vanished for almost the entire document, leaving Lobengula bearing the full burden of the generation, scope and responsibility. Had Rhodes or the authors been more consistently referenced by name, the document would appear to be far less Lobengula-centric and suspicions of European meddling or Lobengula's less than total approval would have been easier to entertain.

The opening phrase, "Know all men," sounds Biblical in its magnificence. Clearly the authors were intending to proclaim a message to a broad scope of men, politicians, barristers, businessmen, prospectors and concession hunters from London to Cape Town. At once grand, the opening phrase could also be read as a warning against any competition. The phrase provides a better understanding of how Rhodes was intending to nullify the competitors in Bulawayo and start the legal and political machinery to the Royal Charter, because it functioned as a "No Trespassing" sign for competition in the entire region.

The grantees are then immediately introduced: Charles Dunell Rudd, Rochfort Maguire and Frances Robert Thompson. As each is named on the very first line of the agreement, they are respectively linked to their cities of origin, Kimberley, London and again, Kimberley. At the time it was a common cultural convention to associate one's name with the city of origin or residence, probably originating from the time of the Norman invasions where the linguistic custom was brought to Saxon England by William the Conqueror. In colonial Africa the practice most likely functioned to anchor citizens of a highly mobile society to their new setting.

In the Rudd Concession, however, the association of the grantees with cities and towns, in the first line especially, serves to associate the grantees individually and collectively not just with Kimberley and London but with *civilization*. To immediately establish them as gentlemen emissaries of Cecil Rhodes and sophisticated Victorian England, of civilized man in fact, the grantees are firmly anchored in the prominent primary position at the beginning of the agreement. "Civilization" then, is a synonym for credibility. Victorians would have been far more apt to believe Rudd, Maguire, and Thompson than a "savage" tyrant ruthlessly ruling one of the most feared and notorious tribes in all of Africa. Civilization not only associates the grantees more closely with the audience, but provides a gloss of authenticity and legitimacy to their claims.

The subtle association with civilization functions by inversely suggesting because Lobengula was not associated with a civilized, modern city he was neither credible nor English-thinking. If one assumes the tone and style serve to subconsciously paint him an educated Englishman by implying he wrote this complicated legalese, then the association with a city reminds the author although the king sounded English and appeared to think like an educated Briton, he was still only a dismissible "savage." This dual message of affirming apparently contradictory claims is ideal for the credulous audience so eager to believe the text. Many key members of the audience *wanted* to believe the Concession because they had vested interests in seeing the agreement approved, and so they needed only weak evidence to persuade.

Lobengula is linked to physical locations in only two instances, both for important legal reasons. On two occasions the Rudd Concession references the "Royal Kraal." Bulawayo was obviously not moveable since it was geographically rooted, but a vague "Royal Kraal" could presumably be erected just about anywhere, a convenient pre-empting should Lobengula be forced out. If he were tied to "the Matabele capital of Bulawayo," then when the Matabele seat would eventually be removed the contract could face annulment or susceptibility to legal wrangling because the hinge-point capital would no longer exist. Keeping in mind that Rhodes always intended to breach this agreement, specifically named capital cities not only sound more legitimate, they sound permanent. The only other reference to Lobengula and a city is in the middle of the text where the authors vaguely define the territory. Although in this instance they include the phrase, "I Lobengula king of Matabeleland Mashonaland and certain adjoining territories," the linking of him to land is made for the far more important purpose of defining in the Concession the broadest expanse of territory the authors could possibly include, for they stood to benefit from vague boundaries. The more land the agreement incorporated, the more likely gold and other mineral wealth would be discovered from which they stood to gain a considerable fortune. Whereas the Rhodes camp is inextricably tied to civilization, Lobengula is only vaguely associated with his "Royal Kraal" and then to his territory in *one* instance, and merely for the purpose of defining the breadth of his kingdom for Rhodes' mineral claim.

After grantees are introduced, the agreement launches into what they will pay him. The sum of one hundred pounds sterling per month in payment for exclusive mineral rights for all of Matabeleland, Mashonaland, and certain adjoining territories is laughable and everyone knew it except the Matabele. By placing the payment so prominently in the Concession, the supposition is not only that Lobengula is being paid generously each and every month, but that his concerns in the bargain are addressed first. The reader is given the impression that after only a few lines the Matabele are already receiving something while the Rhodes camp had received nothing at all, and on top of that they are receiving one hundred pounds sterling every month. If anyone assumes Lobengula authored the document, then the King appears self serving. If they think the Rhodes camp wrote the document, they seem fair and generous.

Over and above this sum of money, the grantees agree to provide one thousand modern Martini-Henry rifles along with suitable ammunition. These were the identical weapons used by the British army. Rhodes knew if anything would seal the agreement, it would be these weapons. Supplying indigenous people with rifles would prove one of the biggest political challenges Rhodes faced in the saga. Arming tribesmen was considered by many settlers to be not only foolish, but criminal because across the entire continent

pockets of colonials could only maintain order and protect themselves by pre-
serving their monopoly of firepower. The Boers even signed a treaty with
Britain forbidding the sale of arms to indigenous people, so the farmers of
Natal, the Orange Free State and the South African Republic were hardly
likely to arm Africans when as farmers they would be the most vulnerable.
Moreover, it would have been unthinkable for Boers to arm people they considered subservient. For the British government even, who would have sup-
plied the weapons to Rhodes, the prospect of supplying modern weapons to
an African tribe gave cause for alarm, hence the need for Rhodes to act sur-
reptitiously. On the other hand, if anyone could deliver the weapons it would
be Rhodes—and Lobengula knew that.

Luckily for Rhodes, powerful politicians supported his goal of seizing the
mining claims for Britain. To many in London, slipping one thousand Martini-Henrys into Bulawayo was a paltry price for such promised mineral
wealth and political maneuvering. Clearly, however, the British government
was concerned the Matabele army would be outfitted with weapons identical
to those fired by the English soldiers, since it was clear the British could very
easily find themselves embroiled in conflict with these warriors. On the other
hand, simply owning a modern weapon does not necessarily make the bearer
a better soldier, as the Matabele realized tragically only too late.

Poignantly missing from the agreement is any reference to training, maintenance, spare parts and future ammunition supplies for the weapons. Unlike
Boer, European and American soldiers and settlers, the Matabele in 1888 had
no substantial prior experience with weapons whatsoever, in that they did not
grow up with them as so many sportsmen and farmers would have. Worse,
they could not even rely upon an industrial-age culture for cross-pollination
of technological familiarity. To educate the Matabele army in their usage
would require extensive and prolonged training. After all, weapons fired haphazardly by untrained solders are worthless; fire power poured by trained soldiers is deadly. Gun sights, for example, require knowledge of distance esti-
mation (in European units of measure), understanding of trajectory and a
great deal of practice. Yet there is no reference to training, maintenance
equipment, or re-supply anywhere. Maintenance of firearms alone in the wet
African climate required specialized knowledge, new mechanical discipline,
and inexhaustible supplies of consumable cleaning agents. Without regular
oiling and cleaning, modern firearms would be unusable. Simply put, Lobengula was being armed with weapons his warriors could neither maintain nor
effectively handle on a battlefield.

Thus, while the British government was apparently contravening various
agreements and common sense by arming the indigenous population, the act
would still substantially benefit the British. As history would later show, the

assumptions of the weapons' ineffectiveness in Matabele hands would play out on the battlefield. When the Matabele did finally end up using their Martini-Henrys in the battles of Bembesi and Shangani in 1893, their lack of training brought tragic results. Many warriors thought the higher they raised their sights the harder the bullets would hit. Still others thought they should "aim" at the bursts of smoke from exploding cannonballs. Not surprisingly, the weapons served only to harm Lobengula's regiments by inducing them to rely on the promise of modern firepower, rather than on their traditional and proven battle tactics. The wasted energy and time of fumbling with unfamiliar mechanisms while drilled maneuvers were abandoned, allowed the Europeans every opportunity to annihilate the impis. Even if one factors in a European bias, the casualty records at the Battle of Bembesi speak for themselves: Indigenous casualties, 3,000, European casualties, four dead and five wounded.

Along with the one hundred pounds sterling a month and one thousand rifles with ammunition, there was a final component in the Rudd Concession for Lobengula. He could choose either an armed steamboat on the Zambezi River or a one-time payment of five-hundred pounds sterling. As with so many tenets of the Rudd Concession, the steamboat delivers far less on a river than appears on paper. The issue of translation is especially poignant in this instance, because the cultural, language and technological divide between the Matabele and Rhodes camp was so immense only an unbiased, truly honest translator would know what questions to ask. The size of the steamboat is not defined. How would the Matabele know to ask about size? The operability of such a boat on the Zambezi is not assessed. The British knew that because of rapids and violent whitewater much of the river was not traversable in anything but a shallow canoe. The armament consists vaguely of "guns suitable for defensive purposes." Conceivably "guns" could mean anything from a small .22 caliber hardly capable of killing a man, to large cannons outfitting a Royal Navy vessel. The number of these weapons is not specified either. It is unlikely the Matabele would know even to ask these questions, leaving the integrity of the *true and thorough* translation to the missionary interpreter, the Reverend Charles Helm. Regardless of the size and number of weapons on the steamboat, there is no mention of type or quantity of ammunition. Finally, with regard to both the steamboat and weaponry, it must be assumed the Matabele would likely have within their kingdom personnel trained in the maintenance and upkeep of the weapons, the sophisticated boiler and engine on the steamboat. If Lobengula had chosen the boat, there is no doubt it would have traversed only the few navigable stretches of the Zambezi River. It would have been poorly armed and without spares or training for the personnel. In no time the boat would have run aground or fallen into disrepair.

Again, Rhodes appears to be arming the Africans when in fact he is trading a useless boat for vast potential mineral wealth.

The only time Lobengula is tied to a location of any legal significance, is with the line, "I Lobengula king of Matabeleland Mashonaland and certain adjoining territories." Here the King is not associated with a permanent city but with a sprawling, indistinct, border-less kingdom spreading indeterminately up anywhere from the Cape Colony and the South African Republic, to somewhere in the east, west and north. Far from associating Lobengula with a civilized European center, he is in fact named ruler of what is indeterminate territory. This effort was not simply to dissociate the King from civilization, as previously discussed. The Rhodes camp wanted an agreement over the widest possible territory they could manage, while still writing a document specific enough to be legally binding. Rhodes would hardly settle for all the minerals in Matabeleland and Mashonaland if he could also secure the minerals in "certain adjoining territories" as well, especially if these territories were so vague as to give the grantees virtually unlimited scope to prospect and mine throughout southern Africa!

It is important to note that although the Matabele tightly controlled Matabeleland, many Mashona had seldom even heard of the ferocious tribe from Bulawayo. Far from being King over a neatly defined kingdom, Lobengula was more accurately in control of Matabeleland and various suzerainties, some more frequently plundered than others. Just as he had no right to proclaim himself king over territories he did not actually control, the British had no right to then claim from Lobengula mining rights over the same broad and un-conquered land. Strangely enough, although the Rudd Concession was designed to deceive Lobengula, this short phrase delineating his kingdom actually conferred upon him a much larger kingdom than he actually controlled, a kingdom that was thus validated and recognized by British authority. The phrase is ironical in that it was simultaneously a crucial clause for both parties holding such entirely divergent ambitions. In the end, though, it only substantiated the broadest land claim by the British.

Lobengula's declarative statement, excerpted below, is by far the most important sentence in the agreement, for with it he signed away control of his kingdom, removed himself from power, consigned his people to servitude, and legally ushered in the Europeans to Matabeleland, Mashonaland and certain adjoining territories.

I Lobengula king of Matabeleland Mashonaland and certain adjoining territories in the exercise of my Sovereign powers and in the presence and with the consent of my Council of Indunas do hereby grant and assign unto the said grantees their heirs representatives and assigns jointly and severally the complete and exclusive charge over all metals and minerals situated and contained in my kingdoms Principalities and dominions together with full power to do all things that they may deem necessary to win and procure the same and to hold collect and enjoy the profits and revenue if any derivable from the said metals and minerals subject to the aforesaid payment.

After the scope of his territory is defined in as broad a manner as the authors could manage (i.e. with the words, "in my kingdoms Principalities and dominions"), they carefully construct the rest of the keystone sentence to solely benefit Rhodes by at once specifically and vaguely defining subsequent terms. For example, in the phrase, "do hereby grant and assign unto the said grantees their heirs representatives and assigns jointly and severally," the authors have defined grantees but in that specific definition have been so broad in the boundaries of the territory that Rhodes would have almost unlimited mining rights in southern Africa.

To subtly expand the meaning in the agreement, doublets and triplets of adjectives, nouns and verbs dominate the Rudd Concession. They enhance the meaning in sentences by incrementally elaborating on a definition, explanation and scope. Rudd and Maguire were naturally reluctant to limit the opportunity of the agreement by inserting vocabulary minimizing their claims, especially when they enjoyed the unusual advantage of language monopoly. That is, they knew the legalese would only be read by a European audience not the Matabele who relied on interpreters secretly paid by Rhodes for their translations. The men neatly expanded the scope of the agreement for Rhodes where most advantageous, by including doublets and triplets in English words which while similar in meaning are not synonyms. When the time came for translation, he would have to be skilled enough to differentiate for the Matabele the subtleties and often *cultural* differences imbedded in the definitions of words, presuming of course parallel words existed in Matabele for translation to take place. Even a skilled translator would struggle explaining cultural and linguistic variances in the vocabulary of another language. Presumably since Helm was simply a missionary in Bulawayo, it could be assumed his ability to translate would fall short of modern requirements in circumstances of such gravity where kingdoms and fortunes are at stake. Fortunately for Rhodes, his camp could capitalize on this void by neatly widening the scope of the Concession. Lobengula, on the other hand, at the very most could only hope for a poor rendition in Matabele of the verbatim Rudd Concession.

The first instance of a doublet or a triplet embellishing a phrase is where Lobengula is said to be defining his kingdom as "Matabeleland, Mashonaland and certain adjoining territories." By placing in sequence three terms, the implication of one, single empire is achieved even though he did not control a kingdom of anywhere this extent. Following this example comes the line: "do hereby *grant* and *assign* unto the said grantees their *heirs representatives* and *assigns jointly* and *severally* the *complete* and *exclusive* charge over all *metals* and *minerals situated* and *contained* in my *kingdoms Principalities* and *dominions* together with full power to do all things that they may deem necessary to *win* and *procure* the same and to *hold collect* and *enjoy* the *profits* and *revenue* if any derivable from the said *metals* and *minerals* subject to the aforesaid payment" (italics added). "Grant" and "assign" solidly define Lobengula's commitment in the Rudd Concession; there is no ambiguity over what Lobengula is doing. "Heirs," "representatives" and "assigns," outlines the benefactors present today and for all future generations. "Complete" and "exclusive" are the two words that make Rhodes' claim over Lobengula's kingdom absolute and unassailable. This pairing of words grant Rhodes a monopoly, for there is no room anywhere in that doublet for other owners including Lobengula.

"Metals" and "minerals" allows Rhodes to claim the efforts were for mining and not for politics. "Situated" and "contained" further magnifies the preceding doublet by again isolating Rhodes' claim to the minerals in Lobengula's immense kingdom. The authors are trying to show they are only entitled to minerals, when in fact the kingdom they defined for themselves is so large and their mandate for mining so vague, they would be entitled to all the mineral wealth in Southern Africa above the Cape Colony and South African Republic.

"Win" and "procure" is a seemingly small doublet tacked on to the end of the phrase, "together with full power to do all things that they may deem necessary to." This phrase destroyed the Matabele kingdom. It was these seemingly insignificant few words that allowed Rhodes to do whatever he chose to secure the minerals. If there was gold under the King's hut, Rhodes had the legal right to mine it. The doublet of "win" and "procure" defined the endless scope of what Rhodes was allowed to do to mine his minerals. Without this phrase the agreement would never have been so devastating to Lobengula. Instead Rhodes would have been given a definitive license to mine in a specific area only and thus could have missed crucial mineral veins, had his efforts made vulnerable to competing prospectors, or more likely, given Lobengula political room and time to bargain further at a later date.

Rhodes wanted to appear to help the Matabele by dealing with a major problem in the kingdom in 1888, namely the horde of concession hunters swarming around the capital. Slyly, Maguire and Rudd inserted a clause giving Rhodes the power to, "exclude from my kingdoms principalities and dominions all persons seeking land metals minerals or mining rights therein." Ostensibly the clause seems reasonable: Rhodes has been granted an exclusive concession for minerals in the Matabele kingdom, and so he deserves the right to enforce his concession. Just preceding the above clause is the phrase, "I do hereby authorize the said grantees their heirs, representatives and assigns to take *all necessary* and *lawful* steps to exclude" (italics added). Unbeknownst to Lobengula, the phrase "all necessary and lawful" quietly gave Rhodes the initial drift from mineral exploitation to legal control within Lobengula's very own kingdom. By the stroke of a pen, Rhodes and his BSAC (British South Africa Company) now had the legal right to decide what was "necessary and lawful" to remove any and all mineral competitors in the vast kingdom. Moreover, he could legally determine the "lawful steps," that is, the *legal process* of such a removal. Therefore, the BSAC was the new legal and enforcement body in the Matabele kingdom insofar as the white prospectors were concerned. Lobengula knew Rhodes had the power to remove any troublesome settlers from Matabeleland. What Lobengula signed, though, was a far more serious breach of his own legal, social and military power. Rhodes now shared at least partial power in Matabeleland. With this legal coup d'état, he acquired a mineral monopoly over the entire territory, the rights to do whatever he wished to secure the minerals, and the legal right to determine the law and method of executing his rule over everyone in the domain.

To further legally corral the Matabele, the authors bound Lobengula to supply impis as needed to help Rhodes remove other concession hunters: "I do undertake to render them such needful assistance as they may from time to time require for the exclusion of such persons." Again the Concession seems reasonable from the Matabele perspective, a few warriors here and there to eliminate the settlers who idle would only be an irritation anyway. Thus Rhodes had cleverly written in a legal guarantee of military support. Lobengula would be committed to sending his very own soldiers to help him and the BSAC entrench themselves in Bulawayo. It would be unlikely Lobengula would ever send troops to help them, especially after the duplicity of the agreement was uncovered. Nevertheless, the intent of the authors to wedge themselves into the kingdom is all the more evident with the commitment.

The final portion of the Rudd Concession constitutes legal protection for both Lobengula and Rhodes. Lobengula agreed not to sign mineral or land concessions with any other party unless specifically agreed to by Rhodes. The monopoly was complete. In return, Lobengula was assured he could break the Rudd Concession if the payment of one hundred pounds sterling per month was in arrear for three months. One could be sure that as long as Rhodes had strength in his body the payments would never be late!

The Rudd Concession ends with the date of the signing followed by the signatures of Lobengula, Charles Dunell Rudd, Rochfort Maguire, and Frank Thompson, witnessed by Charles Helm (the Reverend in the pay of Rhodes), and C. D. Dreyer who was a Dutch transport rider in the Rhodes camp. There is nothing especially remarkable about the signatures themselves, except whereas those of the Europeans are sure and carefully formed, Lobengula's "x" is written more as a "+" by his unfamiliar hand. The form of the mark makes little difference to the legality of the contract, but it speaks volumes about the disparate cultural backgrounds and boundless differences between him and the Europeans.

Analysis of Helm's Endorsement from the British Perspective

The Rudd Concession had no legal validation without the critical endorsement from Reverend Charles Helm. It was customary in colonial Africa for a respected third party to endorse legal contracts to negate the numerous false, deceptive, and unauthenticated documents claiming everything in the Continent from mining rights to chieftainships. As Europeans saw it, the African landscape remained dauntingly confusing, with various kings and pretenders vying for borderless kingdoms. With boundaries so moveable, tribal leaders so remote, kingdoms and territories overlapping with competing claims, it was difficult to authenticate contracts. The Grobler Treaty, for example, was written by Kruger himself then authenticated only by Kruger's party, the very group the suspect document heavily favored. Although terms of the treaty were questionable from the outset because it claimed concessions Lobengula would never have made, it was also not endorsed by a neutral third party such as a member of the laity. Without this crucial endorsement the document lacked legitimacy. To secure this legitimacy, incontrovertible authentication was essential.

Without Helms' endorsement the Rudd Concession would never have sustained scrutiny from neither the politicians and liberals in London, nor from the other local prospectors. There was just too much at stake. Helm's endorsement served both as the unassailable stamp of authenticity and integrity for the Concession, and to attest it had been *fully interpreted to Lobengula* and his indunas. The endorsement would remove any suspicion of fraud with the integrity of the church acting as a sort of religious collateral. With so much in question for so many parties in Reverend Helm's pivotal endorsement, surprisingly little was said to question his role. Certainly there was no talk of him being on Rhodes' payroll.

The endorsement was written in the missionary's own hand. Describing the translation for Lobengula and his indunas, Helm wrote on the agreement that it had been "fully interpreted and explained by me to Chief Lobengula and his full Council of Indunas." The phrase "fully interpreted and explained" becomes slippery when the interpreter was in the pay of the grantee. If Helm was translating as accurately and fairly as he could, his phrase assumed his translation accommodates both the language-level and cultural-level understanding. He may well have fully interpreted and explained the agreement as he would to an Englishman. He might have communicated with culturally-familiar metaphors, allusions and semantic synonyms, taking for granted a lifetime of cultural and educational familiarity. For example, when explaining a legally binding agreement to an educated Englishmen, it would probably not be necessary to elaborate that verbal elements—especially if they are crucial concessions—are *not* legally binding in an English courtroom if they are left out of the written agreement. With Lobengula, though, such cultural assumptions cannot and should not have been made. This endorsement and translation it describes became pivotally questionable when one remembers the signing of the Concession resulted in Lobengula losing his kingdom. Unless one is to believe Lobengula willingly signed away his power and people for the sake of one hundred pounds sterling a month and a thousand rifles, it is implausible to believe the Rudd Concession had been, "fully interpreted and explained by me to Chief Lobengula and his full Council of Indunas."

Helm certainly explained and interpreted the agreement in some way, for Lobengula felt secure enough to sign on October 30, 1888. Yet he must not have bridged the cavernous cultural divide between an illiterate King in Matabeleland and literate barristers in England. To be as generous as possible to Helm, there may have been difficulty in finding equivalent vocabulary to translate the wording. Illiterate Matabeles could have had difficulty in understanding the absoluteness of the phrase, "with full power to do all things that they may deem necessary to win and procure the same." They had no real concept of individual land ownership and no familiarity with the nuances of the English language where the simple word "all" translates into the Rhodes camp having legal power and right to determine *any* means of their choosing.

Metaphor was a common device of translation at the time when cultural synonyms did not exist. The problem with metaphor is by its very nature the literal is converted to an abstract, often with just as many pits of interpretation and understanding being formed in the effort to clarify. Whether deliberately or inadvertently, the explanation almost certainly muddied understanding. Metaphors and devices of explanation can be purposely confusing, deliberately simplistic and misleading, or simply poor usages that without any dishonest intent fail to clarify the situation. No transcript of Helm's interpretation of the Rudd Concession to Lobengula exists, so references to earlier interpretations from the Rhodes camp have to be made in order to distill likely scenarios of understanding. In discussions leading to the signing of the agreement when Thompson was imploring Lobengula to grant a concession to only one group, the Englishman explained that he did not want to have two

bulls in a single herd of cows. The explanation is framed to clarify by referencing a familiar and fundamental facet of Matabele life, their livestock.
Thompson compares the problems of granting a concession to two competing
parties, with two bulls competing over cows in a herd. Superficially, this may
be an apt metaphor since no doubt bulls would vigorously compete over cows
at the expense of peace in the herd. The metaphor ceases to be relevant and
informative after superficial analysis, since what Thompson was really after
was not just exclusive procreation with the cows, but any and all conceivable
means to procreate. Thompson wanted exclusive use of the cows for prolifer-
ation, and for the eventual harvesting of their hides, meat and milk, not to
mention control over the fields in which they roamed and rivers from where
they drank. A bull in a herd of cows may be the sole progenitor of subsequent
generations, though neither the bull nor its herdsman would ever conceive of
the animal doing anything more than simply providing genetic continuation.
Thus the superficiality of such an interpretation illustrates how some meaning, some explanation, some understanding was provided to Lobengula, but
by no means was the explanation complete especially when the issue at stake
was a kingdom and its citizens. Thompson's metaphor, as was Helm's no
doubt, is better described as a surface-level story detailing fractional elements
of the agreement.

Since it is impossible to believe Helm thought Lobengula and his indunas
properly understood the ramifications of the Rudd Concession, Helm's endorsement is completely false. He may have provided *an* interpretation un-
derstandable by an Englishman or barrister, but clearly there was no adequate
explanation of this Concession, again, unless one is to believe that Lobengula
willingly signed away his kingdom. Explanations rise above interpretations,
for the former remain squarely within the domain of the subjective ("Rudd's
interpretation of the agreement," or "Reverend Helm's interpretation of the
Concession"), whereas the latter bridge from the subjective understanding to
the objective, spanning whatever cultural, linguistic or educational boundaries dividing the two parties. An explanation extends out of the realm of the
self into the conception of the addressee, in this case Lobengula and his indunas. It must rise above assumption, self-focus, conjecture or limitations of
most kinds to provide full understanding of the issue from the context and
perspective of the person hearing the explanation. If Helm truly explained the
Rudd Concession he might well have used metaphor or any other device of
communication, but he would not have stopped his effort until Lobengula understood it in *Matabele terms*. Whether for reasons of personal financial
gain or to improve the pasture for proselytizing to "save" heathen Matabele,
the latter being the more likely reason, Helm's endorsement may have been

justified to him on a Machiavellian ends-justify-the-means rationale. For most people, however, it was a deliberate deception.

LOBENGULA'S INTERPRETATION

To analyze Lobengula's interpretation of the Concession requires the analyst to rely more heavily on supposition than with Rhodes' interpretation. No one can claim absolute knowledge of Rhodes' intentions, but there is considerably more information from his own writing, memoirs, accounts, as well as an extensive body of literature to substantiate claims of his intentions. The Matabele were illiterate, however. Whatever little correspondence from Bulawayo was recorded has been heavily factored into this examination, yet it must be made clear that information is scant. Nevertheless, almost all accounts of what Lobengula and his indunas "said" come from the writing of Rhodes' emissaries or other Europeans in varying distances from the Rhodes epicenter. Details about Lobengula's thoughts, conversations and actions must of course then be treated with a measure of diligence and suspicion. In determining Lobengula's interpretation, references to an extensive body of literature where source materials have been analyzed and evaluated against each other to form a likely consensus, and have been the principal foundation for the assumptions inherent in interpreting the actions of an illiterate king.

Common sense and probability—however culturally situated they may be—also played a vital role in determining the King's probable interpretations. Based on all available sources, it is assumed Lobengula was always acting in the best interests of his people and not prompted by motives of self preservation or enrichment; there is no evidence to point to the contrary and it would been highly unlikely for a king so dependent on his subjects. This assumption is based on conclusions ascertained from a thorough reading of contemporary writing and modern analyses of the period, in which there is not a word to suggest Lobengula ever acted upon selfish motives. Nevertheless, the interpretation is still an assumption based upon purported facts, memoirs, verbal accounts and academic findings spanning the gamut of bias. Every effort has been made to determine Lobengula's *probable* interpretation. However, it is conceded that whatever conclusions are drawn will inevitably be based upon information almost exclusively *not* Matabele in origin. All such conclusions must be viewed through a lens of academic rigor in which sources remain open for analysis.

Discussion of Lobengula's interpretation of the Rudd Concession must begin with clarification of the content of the agreement itself, insofar as Lobengula was concerned. Shortly after arriving in Bulawayo the Rhodes camp realized they were not going to persuade him to sign anything without further promises to assuage his fears that his people would be harmed by a contract with the Europeans. If Rudd, Maguire and Thompson hoped to secure Lobengula's signature on the Concession, they would have to convince a wily, nervous King that he would be fully protected.

The Matabele relied upon an oral tradition for record keeping and tribal memory. The memories of most Matabeles was generally superb, Lobengula's in particular because as King he needed to remember the numerous royal proceedings taking place in Bulawayo, not to mention the fact that a king with a poor memory in an oral culture would be vulnerable to manipulation. The spoken word was as sacrosanct and as legally binding as any written word in the English courtroom. The Rhodes camp knew they could make verbal promises to entice them, because officials in Bulawayo would assume the verbal agreements as binding as the written, if not more so. Rudd, Maguire and Thompson knew well the verbal promises would merely function as a catalyst to the signing, but were of no legal merit whatsoever. The strategy was ideal for Rhodes because it would seduce Lobengula and the Matabele while placing the Rhodes camp at no further liability.

The Matabele had little choice but to place faith in trusted interpreters. With no inkling their primary trusted interpreter was in the pay of Rhodes, they would never suspect portions of the agreement benefiting them most were simply legal fabrications. The promises were of no more relevance in an English courtroom than conjecture, supposition, or hearsay. Cleverly Rudd and Maguire defined the portions of the contract crucial for Rhodes, in plain, *written* legal terms valid in any courtroom. Lobengula's inducements, the sections that mattered to him most but were detrimental to Rhodes' vision, were neatly given *verbally* to maximize persuasion in the Royal Kraal without contaminating the Rudd Concession in England. The problem for Lobengula, was his audience was not the Matabele who would dwell more heavily on the verbal promises, but the Europeans in London and the Cape who focused on the text.

Lobengula's interpretation of the Rudd Concession was upon the written concession as already outlined, along with the following key verbal promises:

1. No more than 10 men would dig in his country at any time.
2. They would dig only one hole or in only one place.
3. There would be no digging near towns.
4. The diggers would be as Lobengula's own subjects.
5. The white miners would fight in defense of the kingdom if called upon (Thomas 196).

Insofar as he was concerned, the verbal promises *were* the Rudd Concession. The promises that inducing him to sign what was otherwise a rather lopsided and vague agreement were fundamental. As the written document stood, Lobengula refused to sign it. By the admission of Helm and other members of the Rhodes camp, the verbal promises were then added after the document was drafted in an effort to induce him to sign. This being true, the verbal promises were a critical part of Lobengula's Concession, making the misrepresentation a profound deceit.

Analysis of the Verbal Promises

In the first verbal promise the number of miners allowed to dig is so small any historian can be sure Rudd never intended for the promises to leave Bulawayo or be honored in any way. Considering the labor, logistical support and management necessary for even a small mining operation, limiting the number of digging men to ten would hardly be worth the effort for a mining magnate on Rhodes' scale. This first verbal concession was crucial to Lobengula, because it offered an assurance that should he be duped in the agreement, at least he would only have to contend with ten Europeans at a time. Ten miners would be a manageable number.

The second verbal promise, that *miners would dig only one hole or only in one place at a time*, would also have been impossible for Rhodes to honor, because to make any viable mining venture would require extensive prospecting over the full range of the Matabele kingdom. If as hoped Matabeleland and Mashonaland were the continuation of a vast mineral belt, it is safe to say Rhodes would dig more than one hole and in more than one place. It is likely that if he found such a rich site he could mine at that site only, presuming the phrase "dig only one hole or in only one place" would mean the size of the one hole could be the acreage of a city. The pit mine at Kimberley remains to this day the largest man made hole in the world! No one knows how big Lobengula imagined a mine consisting of one hole or in one place, manned by only ten men would be, but it is safe to assume he felt he would control it effectively.

The third promise that there *would be no digging near towns* is one Rhodes would have honored, because he was shrewd enough to know that keeping his men and activities isolated from the already aggravated Matabele would benefit all involved. He did not want to prolong chafing the indigenous people, especially the volatile matjaha. On the other hand, if a rich mineral belt running square through Lobengula's royal kraal were discovered, somehow the royal seat would certainly be moved elsewhere.

Lobengula did not want any miners at all. If he was to have them, and he knew inevitably he would have to tolerate some, at least the verbal promises would keep the disruption to his people's independence and traditions to a minimum. By keeping miners away from towns, he hoped to limit the interaction

between the whites and his impis. Even interactions between miners and his ordinary citizens could flare up with one side accusing the other of theft or en-
croachment. Keeping miners and Matabele far apart would ensure a longer,
more peaceful coexistence.

The fourth verbal promise was any *miners would live in Matabeleland as
Lobengula's own subjects*, meaning they were not an autonomous, independent
body occupying land, but be bound and obligated to follow Lobengula as any
Matabele subject. He could not tolerate sharing power since his authority was
derived from an absolute right to rule. Unfortunately no one pointed out that the
fourth verbal promise directly contradicted two tenets of the written agreement.
In the middle of the Concession is the following line, "[I] do hereby grant and
assign unto the said grantees their heirs representatives and assigns jointly and
severally the *complete and exclusive charge* over all metals and minerals situated and contained in my kingdoms Principalities and dominions" (italics
added). If the miners have complete and exclusive charge over the mineral
wealth, then how can they also be subjects of the King? Immediately after this
line comes the following phrase further undermining the verbal agreement, "together with *full power to do all things that they may deem necessary to win and
procure the same*" (italics added). In fact, "together with full power to do all
things that they may deem necessary to win and procure the same" gives Rhodes
and the miners the power to do virtually anything they wanted in the territory,
regardless of Lobengula, his indunas or their impis.

The fifth verbal promise was for *the white miners to fight in defense of the
Matabele kingdom should Lobengula be attacked*. The fifth promise was easy
for Rhodes to honor, since it was in his very best interests to defeat any aggressors against the Matabele because his interests were now part of their
kingdom. Of course this loyalty assumes the aggressor was someone other
than Rhodes. The Matabele were not usually the subject of offensive attack
from traditional enemies. The real fear in Bulawayo was Boer incursions;
Lobengula hoped this clause would serve as a means of ensuring British protection against such an invasion. Ironically though, what Bulawayo leadership did not seem to fully realize was that their greatest threat was from the
very person with whom they were striking the agreement.

With the exception of the fifth promise, the verbal concessions were clearly
added by Rhodes only to mollify Lobengula and his indunas and never meant
to be honored. They were hopelessly unacceptable in any real or legalistic sense
to the magnate because they would have kept his grand mining ambitions at
such a minuscule level that the entire venture would be worthless. The first two
promises especially, those limiting the diggers to ten men working in one place
only, were antithetical to Rhodes' ambitions of having exclusive and total control of mining territory in Matabeleland. There simply would be no point in

having such a large claim if the grantees were then to be limited and hobbled in carrying on the mining itself. For this reason the verbal clauses were undoubtedly made only to secure and not to honor the agreement.

Unlike so many other facets of the Concession signing where Rhodes was acting deceptively, it is Lobengula who was negligent with the verbal promises. He and his indunas cannot claim the inaccuracies to be the fault of poor translation or complications of legalese, but a lapse in their own common sense. Regardless of who was translating, the motives of the translator, or gaps in cultural relativity, the fundamentals of the written Rudd Concession and the verbal promises have never been in doubt: Rhodes wanted exclusive mineral rights to Lobengula's entire kingdom and all means to secure the minerals. Even if Lobengula did not understand the details of the written agreement, he knew Rhodes was after exclusive mining rights to his territory. Insofar as the verbal promises go, the King was under no misapprehension about their details since he referenced them in various letters written after the signing. If he understood only that the magnate was after a monopoly of mining rights in his territory, and Rhodes had agreed to the five verbal promises which limited the operability of his mining monopoly, it is Lobengula and his indunas who must hold some blame for not using more common sense in seeing the essence of the written and verbal Rudd Concession were incompatible. If one man wants to mine in Matabeleland, Mashonaland and certain adjoining territories—and mine exclusively—but he then also agrees to dig only one hole or mine in one place with no more than ten men, then either the man intends to capitalize on the vast mineral wealth slowly or he is lying and intends to bring in an army of miners. Moreover, if Rudd had spent close to three months negotiating exclusive mining rights, if that exclusivity was so sought after for him to pursue it doggedly under such tense and frightening circumstances, it goes without saying the verbal promises hamstringing the broad written concession would be broken. Certainly Rhodes, Maguire, Rudd and Thompson merit no credit for their gross misrepresentation. It is Lobengula, though, as protector of his people who ultimately bore the greatest responsibility to have detected the mutually incompatible facets of the written and verbal contracts.

LANGUAGE AND THE MONOPOLY OF KNOWLEDGE

"Ipsa scientia potestas est"—"knowledge itself is power". If ever Francis Bacon's maxim was true, it was here in 1888 when the knowledge of language was the power. Just as shrewd tactics defeated Roman legions at the Battle of Teutoburger Wald in 9AD, and the longbow triumphed over armored cavalry at Agincourt in 1415, the knowledge of written language overwhelmed the

Matabele in 1888. Rhodes held a monopoly on language in the development, signing and implementation of this plan. His emissaries drafted the agreement, his translator interpreted the agreement, and his audience enacted the agreement. Not only did Lobengula not know the English language, he did not know English conventions. Rhodes held an immeasurable advantage over the Matabele, for he drafted a legal document imbedded with socio-cultural idiosyncrasies and jargon as foreign and incomprehensible to Lobengula as cultural nuances in Bulawayo would be to any Londoner at the time.

The language void left the burden of understanding squarely with Lobengula. Although the document was written by Rudd and Maguire to sound as though drafted by Lobengula, the King understood only what was explained to him. All Lobengula could rely upon was his common sense and the integrity of the translator, Reverend Helm, such as it was. Unfortunately for him, unlike on the battlefields of Southern Africa where advantages with warriors, terrain, and weaponry are immediately palpable, the King found himself making a decision for his kingdom based on instinct and the incomplete translation of a missionary. He had everything to lose. Even if he did well in the contract, he could at best only hope to maintain a weak control over the region from that time onwards. It was unlikely his kingdom could develop quickly enough to properly and sustainably defend itself from the new outsiders. If he did badly, though, he lost his throne and the independence of a hundred thousand Matabele subjects. Rhodes' vision for the Cape-to-Cairo railway running squarely though Matabeleland was conceived years before the signing in 1888. Whereas Lobengula had to guess at the next frame in the drama of Southern Africa, Rhodes merely consulted his blueprints. All Lobengula could do was respond to Rhodes' actions, never shape the course of events himself. The fly waited helplessly as the chameleon edged closer.

ROLE OF THE MISSIONARIES

The role of the missionaries in Matabeleland lays bare the troubling semantics behind the proselytizing efforts of religious groups in Southern Africa. The mandate from the English Christians via the LMS was for missionaries to penetrate the continent, Christianize the Africans, and bring salvation to what they saw as the otherwise damned people of Africa. The problem there, as elsewhere, was Lobengula refused the idea of having his people worship any other "king". Even though he always treated the missionaries with unusual kindness and respect, going so far as to consider Robert Moffat something of a father-figure, they were spectacularly unsuccessful around Bulawayo. Nevertheless, missionaries remained in the fold becoming highly trusted interpreters and emissaries for the King.

Unfortunately for the missionaries, they were still unable to convert a single Matabele, let alone an entire tribe. After decades of failure and no respite anywhere on the horizon, it became clear to the LMS, Charles Helm and other missionaries in the field, that unless Lobengula was removed from power and the existing Matabele order crushed, the proselytizing effort would continue to fail. Herein lies the problem: the Bible strictly forbids murder, lying and deception, yet commands followers to spread the Word. If by spreading the Word many thousands of otherwise "damned" Matabele could be saved and the "open sore of the world" in Matabeleland could be healed, then just as killing in war is euphemized and re-classified as a necessary undertaking, a just and perhaps even noble *duty*, then surely too the same justification of semantics could be applied to "saving" the Matabele. Ordinarily, lying, deceit and murder would be wrong. If committed in the name of the Lord for a much greater good, then a compelling case could be made that it was in fact one's duty as a Christian to overthrow the King to save the other 100,000 Matabele.

So the drama unfolded in Matabeleland upon the apparently divergent paths of gold and the gospel, which for a time surprisingly converged upon the same goal of toppling the Matabele order. The alliance of Rhodes and missionaries upon initial examination appears to have been unlikely, yet both groups ultimately sought power, one spiritual the other temporal.

CONCLUSION TO THE ANALYSIS

The rhetorical examination of the Rudd Concession yields a document carefully crafted to deceive Lobengula into signing away his kingdom, while convincing an albeit receptive European audience to accept Lobengula willingly conceded power. What makes it so extraordinary is not so much the enormous scope of the agreement, but how simple were the language and tactics to yield one of the most comprehensive land grants in history. The Rudd Concession was not a perplexing muddle of legal terms or confusing double entendre. The agreement remains an extraordinary enigma of law and conquest, because through rather ordinary deception and manipulation of information Rhodes seized from one of the most intelligent and wily rulers in Southern Africa a kingdom the size of Australia.

The rhetorical analysis of the Rudd Concession reveals more about the environment in which the document was conceived than anything momentous in the language itself. Language-level analysis of the document shows a carefully orchestrated legal coup d'état in which syntax and figures of speech painstakingly propagated for Lobengula a mirage of bounty, the Concession itself merely the signifier of a far greater deception. It was the last formal step in an elaborate production of missionaries, translators, government officials and speculators banding together to deceive the Matabele and filch their land.

The agreement, moreover, would not have been signed but for almost unparalleled alliances drawn behind the scenes. High ranking politicians in England, key politicians like Shippard in the Cape, speculators and missionaries, most with vastly disparate agendas, came together to topple the Matabele order. This co-operation to remove a common obstacle makes the Rudd unique. Representing the British government, had Shippard not so earnestly urged Lobengula to sign only with the largest company, Lobengula would probably not have signed. If Helm had maintained his integrity in securing his goal of converting the Matabele, and not reverted to such dubious means, would Lobengula have signed? Even if members of the Rhodes camp, Maguire, Thompson and Rudd had given in to Lobengula accepting a joint concession with another company, as they very nearly did, would Lobengula's kingdom have stayed intact a little longer? The tide had turned against the Matabele and their destiny was inevitable—whether this turn took place with Rhodes or someone else soon after.

This Concession was the portal to power in Matabeleland. New paths were laid for all future temporal and spiritual endeavors. The agreement exists in history not as a rhetorical masterpiece defeating the wits of a capable adversary, but as the manifestation of the ambitions promoted by antithetical groups seeking to deceive and beguile through a coordinated monopoly of knowledge. The treaty remains an apotheosis of opportunity spawning a collusion of interests acting together on Machiavellian impulses. For the Matabele and what would become Rhodesia, it was a turning point marking the introduction of formalized colonization and Europeanization of the region that has lasted in various forms and through continuing conflict to this day. As Lobengula had anxiously envisioned so long before, the chameleon had swallowed the fly.

NOTE

1. The whereabouts of the original Rudd Concession are uncertain. The document was supposedly lost when its caretaker forgot it in a taxi cab on the way back from having it photographed.

Chapter Five

Conclusion

As the final pages of this book are written, the waning days of colonial involve-ment in Zimbabwe's land crisis—the culmination of the Rudd Concession—are drawing to a close. Over the past decade, Prime Minister Robert Mugabe and ruling party ZANU PF members have "won" most seats in elections condemned as fraudulent by nearly all Western countries and, surprisingly, by many African nations. The platform against the opposition party Movement for Democratic Change (M.D.C.) was ostensibly based upon ZANU PF's on-going land reform program, whereby the Zimbabwe government would seize white-owned farms and redistribute them to Zimbabwe's sixty percent unemployed. The official ra-tionale is that because land was seized illegally by Europeans in the 1888 Rudd Concession and 1889 Royal Charter, it was simply being returned to its "origi-nal owners," presuming them to be the descendants of the 1888 Mashonas and Matabele.

Most scholars and economists agree the current land seizure program has less to do with land rights and wealth equity than a crude attempt to maintain polit-ical power. After twenty-seven years of deficit spending, unabashed corruption and economic policies designed to favor the autocracy, Zimbabwe has fallen from being called the breadbasket of Africa to indisputably having the world's worst economy. Land predominantly owned by the small minority of white farmers has been seized by the government and redistributed almost exclusively to a handful of black government supporters, this under the banner of redress-ing the Rudd Concession and other colonial injustices. The iconic power of the land question was the rallying cry bringing Mugabe to power in the first place. Ironically, and cruelly for the Zimbabwean people, it remains a rallying cry of the government, but this time to keep itself in power at the expense of the citizenry—white and black alike. Few issues remain so resoundingly volatile as the land distribution legacy from the colonial era. For this reason land's iconic status remains ripe for contemporary political manipulation.

Land is a finite resource. Each group will fight to the death for their share and winner takes all. What then for the losers? Whether it was territory occupied by the Khoisan then taken by the first settlers in the Cape in 1652, fields owned by the various small tribes in Natal and overrun by the raiding Zulu in the early nineteenth century, Matabeleland taken by the Europeans under the Rudd Concession in 1888, or white farms now seized by Mugabe's government and given to party loyalists in the land seizure era of the early 2000 period, the question of land ownership in Zimbabwe, in Africa, and elsewhere in the world remains the fulcrum of so many power struggles. A history of Africa and the analysis of the Rudd Concession are a study of land conflict. To understand land in Africa is to understand the continent's past, present and future. What, then, does the Concession mean for current politics in Southern Africa? What role does it play and has its legacy been redressed?

The land situation is as chaotic as ever. If anything is clear, it is that many of the accusations levied against colonials of the nineteenth century can still be made today, only this time against many nationalist black leaders. Certainly the colonials exploited indigenous people by forcefully taking their land, goading the population into the workforce, then relying on threats and brutality to enforce government rule. Corruption and cruelty existed at the highest levels of government. The very principles of "salvation" and "civilization" imposed by the colonial governments and missionaries were misguided and arrogant. Yet paradoxically, these same principles are being followed by the very same black leaders in Zimbabwe today, most of whom rose to powerful positions on a tide of reform from the colonial era. These self-styled liberation figures grew up in the same huts as did their citizens, fought the same struggles, suffered under the same rule. Despite their shared legacy, they have emerged as dictators and autocrats to dominate and control their own people with a rare ferocity. President Mugabe in Zimbabwe is a particularly severe example of this phenomenon. Whether it is subjugation and exploitation of the indigenous people in the Victorian era by the Europeans, or subjugation of the Africans today by their own leaders, little has changed politically in some parts of Africa over the past two centuries. While the Rudd Concession as an agreement has become an almost forgotten footnote in history, resurrected only when politically expedient, the politics behind the agreement and the collusion it engenders still dominates Zimbabwean politics.

For all that can be written about the Concession, two facts remain clear. The legacy of the document is as volatile today as it ever was. As troubling, the confluence of social, political and economic factors that created it originally, are at this moment forming successors to the agreement. There is a farm just outside Harare where the untilled land was cleared and prepared for large-scale agriculture in 1927 by one of the thousands of British colonials settling in early Rhodesia. For three generations the farm remained in the hands of the original settler family. The farm employed one hundred and fifty workers, many of whom are descendants of original families living there before the colonials arrived. Each year it purchased hundreds of thousands of dollars of supplies from a myriad of businesses, paid taxes to the government, housed and employed over one hundred families, and grew exportable crops sold in international markets to earn foreign currency for the nation. By all measures, the farm was a highly productive and successful commercial enterprise.

In March 2003, the final step in Mugabe's land seizure program reached this farm when it was "pegged" into plots purportedly for allocation to the nearly sixty percent unemployed in Zimbabwe. This moment could be a final phase in the legacy of the Rudd Concession, or more plausibly a contemporary reincarnation of it. It is no surprise to anyone closely monitoring the political schemes and corruption commonplace in Africa today, to know the farm was *not* allocated to landless Africans. One large portion was been claimed by a colonel in the Zimbabwe army, another by a high ranking member of ZANU-PF, while still another large portion went to a senior member of the Central Intelligence Organization (CIO). Instead of being parceled out to the landless, it was given as a reward to cronies and party faithful. It was also a bid by the government to silence political opposition seen to be arising from white commercial farmers and their black farm workers. One immediate and terrible ramification on this farm alone was the displacement of the hundreds who worked and lived on this land for generations. Most farm workers were forced to move elsewhere, yet they have nowhere to go and little chance of securing work anywhere in the country with sixty percent unemployment. Mugabe's scheme displaces far more currently employed people than giving land and work to the unemployed. Compounding the problem, farming supply business infrastructure such as tractor companies, fertilizer producers, and other support companies have gone out of business because the commercial farms were destroyed. Subsistence level plots are too small for mechanization and seldom economically viable enough to afford fertilizers and pesticides. The job displacement ricochets around the country putting more and more companies out of business as agriculture, previously one of the country's major industries, collapses completely. As most of the commercial farms are now broken up, Zimbabwe faces its first famine after a century of plentiful food. The erstwhile "breadbasket of Africa" now desperately seeks international aid to *import* food for the 7.8 million of the country's 13 million citizens going hungry.

A final insult to those displaced by Mugabe's scheme, and a final insult to the many millions of Zimbabweans facing this once unheard-of famine, is that most of the newly allocated farms now owned by Mugabe's faithful are not being farmed at all. Once stripped of salable assets such as tractors and irrigation equipment, these trophy farms grow nothing but weeds in the soil. Roads are washed out, top soil silts the rivers, and farm buildings lie derelict. Once verdant fields are now wastelands. Regionally, similar notions of land reform are extending to neighboring countries such as South Africa, Botswana and Zambia. In the mean time, these countries are suffering from an exodus of Zimbabweans desperate for food, housing and jobs since the farm worker evictions.

Facing this national disintegration, it is important to recognize the distinction between the original legacy of the agreement and the modern legacy. The original is one marked by a hundred years of genuine land inequity, in which a small minority of the population controlled the most productive land. This disparity was the manifestation of practical economic considerations predicated on maintaining wealth and privilege for the white minority population. White social and political movements were thus entrenched in maintaining this privileged status. Likewise, the black population recognized the social, economic and political disparity and became equally determined to see its demise. Both sides, however, were committed to the land itself, by either maintaining or acquiring control of it. So strong were these convictions, only the bloody war of independence in the 1970s and global economic sanctions against the Rhodesian government could force a resolution.

The countervailing legacy of the Rudd Concession is contemporary and far removed from the racial bifurcation or true ownership of resources. It has become purely abstract politically with little relation to ideological land ownership. Considering the current government came to power principally through the rallying cry of land reform, the original legacy of the Concession, it is deeply ironic the same government has not only failed to address the inequities, but has actually re-defined these colonial legacies to suit their present political agenda. In light of policies whereby farms have been seized and redistributed mostly to government supporters, a practice suspiciously akin to the early colonial period, the government can hardly rally behind the nationalist cause of true land reform. How can they if the seized land is re-distributed to this small all-powerful black autocracy? Instead of substantive and grounded policy change, the government touts the emotive, iconic and increasingly hollow rhetoric of addressing "colonial legacies" and preventing neo-imperialism. Few foreign governments, let alone Zimbabweans themselves, see contemporary politics, and especially the land reform movement, as being anything but practical politicking that has for convenience and expediency hitched itself to a newly fabricated colonial legacy. Land is power—governments know it—and thus control of it by the government is the key to political longevity in Zimbabwe.

The final chapter in the Rudd Concession saga is the rather cynical realization that little has ultimately changed in Zimbabwe's land legacy since the signing of the Concession in 1888. In the 1890s land ownership was transferred from the weaker indigenous land owners to the new foreign ruling elite minority. A look at the land ownership claims in Zimbabwe today will show the same ownership of a ruling elite minority, but this time of black government officials and supporters. The entire colonization effort was an exercise in adaptability: Rhodes was able to adapt whereas Lobengula was ultimately unable to control and shape events to his own advantage. Today President Mugabe and other African leaders enjoy all the vices once derided in the imperialists. The very leaders who ousted the white regimes now own gold and diamond mines throughout Africa. In fact, large diamond reserves, possibly some of the richest discovered anywhere in the past decade, have recently been located in eastern Zimbabwe. They are currently the subject of fierce fighting amongst top-level ZANU PF officials scrambling to gain larger shares of the vast wealth. As expected, little has trickled down to benefit most Zimbabweans and certainly nothing has been given to the nation. How ironic that Rhodes and his contemporaries staked their fortunes and labored so tirelessly to find great mineral wealth in this part of the world, only to conclude that mineral resources were scant and the land was best suited for farming. Now, a century later, some of the best farmland in the world is idle and diamond fever has gripped the nation!

For all criticisms levied against Rhodes and his contemporaries, many of which are deserved for they were truly dishonest with Lobengula, they did build a nation as they sought great wealth for themselves. Rhodesia's substantial infrastructure, agricultural industry, education system and medical services are evidence of this nation-building, albeit that some resources were largely intended for the white minority. At the very least, bequeathed philanthropic gifts from these individuals continue to serve and enrich countless individuals in Zimbabwe and across the world. Out of many examples, the Birchenough Bridge and Beit Halls were given in the name of Alfred Beit for infrastructure development and education programs. Rhodes scholarships annually fund approximately ninety students from countries worldwide to study at the University of Oxford. It is true that some philanthropists from that era intended to primarily benefit white people. On the other hand, those giving to the nation as a whole with no racial prejudice are far more frequent. What these benefactors had in common was a fundamental belief in creating a nation, in a giving back to their communities, and in providing for the less fortunate.

I make this point not to defend Rhodes but to highlight the incongruity, national tragedy, and outright hypocrisy of the current leadership. Out of their wealth, what have they given to the nation, to their people? Unlike Rhodes, the ruling echelon came to power promising to eradicate a system they found oppressive and yet have ultimately embraced that system and taken its repressive steps farther. Is it worse for black Zimbabweans to not have the right to vote, or to have that right only to see their government violently target anyone voting against them? Is it progress to be able to own land where they please, only for the government to forcefully seize their farms and assets if the move proves politically expedient? With the experience of having lived under colonialism, and having had the power since he became Prime Minister to make substantive changes for the better, Robert Mugabe's legacy is one of pillage, exploitation and waste. Examples of their excess are so numerous and flagrantly carried out volumes would be necessary to catalogue them. Indeed, the Rudd Concession has provided a legacy of distrust and squandered opportunities.

After 120 years, where are we now? Rhodes was hardly more predatory than many businessmen today, and no different from Mugabe who seized power fighting his institutions. He was just more successful, better at conquering others, and thus has been singled out as the archetypal imperialist. In his footsteps and by taking many pages from his book, have come legions of new "imperialists"—only this time waving different flags, decrying other histories, and just as self-assured in their ideologies. Despite the lessons from the Rudd Concession, and in view of the crises overwhelming Africa to this day, the final significance of the agreement is a resounding affirmation of Darwinian opportunism. Every age has its flies and chameleons. Graft and corruption are always with us and so the world goes on. Indeed, every man seems to have his price.

Bibliography

Africa 1853. Map. Boston: Jenks, Hickling and Swan, 1853.

Africa 1877. Map. Wilson, Hinkle and Co, 1877.

Africa 1885. Map. James Monteith, 1855.

Becker, Peter. *Path of Blood: The Rise and Conquests of Mzilikazi Founder of the Matabele Tribe of Southern Africa*. London: Longmans, Green and Co. Ltd, 1962.

Blake, Robert. *A History of Rhodesia*. New York: Alfred A. Knopf, Inc, 1978.

Clement, A. J. "The Incidents Leading to the Death of Lobengula's Indunas, 1893." *Africana Notes and News* 17.2 (1966): 80–83.

Cobbing, J. R. D. "The Unknown Fate of the Rudd Concession Rifles." *Rhodesian History* 3 (1972): 77–81.

Dodds, Glen Lyndon. *The Zulus and Matabele Warrior Nations*. London: Arms and Armour Press, 1998.

Edmond, John. *The Battle of Bembezi*. Roan Antelope Music.

FitzPatrick, J. Percy. *Through Mashonaland with Pick and Pen*. 1892. Ed. A. P. Cartwright. Johannesburg: AD, Donker, 1973.

Galbraith, John S. *Crown and Charter: The Early Years of the British South Africa Company*. Berkeley: University of California Press, 1974.

Gann, L. H., and Peter Duignan. *Burden of Empire: An Appraisal of Western Colonialism in Africa South of the Sahara*. New York: Frederick A. Praeger, 1967.

Gann, L. H. *A History of Southern Rhodesia: Early Days to 1934*. London: Chatto & Windus, 1965.

Gann, L. H., and M. Gelfand. *Huggins of Rhodesia: The Man and His Country*. London: George Allen & Unwin Ltd, 1964.

Hassing, Per. "Lobengula." *Leadership in Eastern Africa: Six Political Biographies*. Ed. Norman R. Bennett. Boston: Boston UP, 1968. 223–260.

Knight-Bruce, G. W. H. (Bishop). "The Mashonaland Mission of Bishop Knight-Bruce." In *Gold and the Gospel in Mashonaland 1888*. Oppenheimer Series 4. London: Chatto and Windus, 1949.

Mason, Philip. *The Birth of a Dilemma: The Conquest and Settlement of Rhodesia*. London: Oxford UP, 1958.

Morris, Donald R. *The Washing of the Spears*. New York: Simon & Schuster, Inc, 1965.

Mutambirwa, James A. Chamunorwa. *The Rise of Settler Power in Southern Rhodesia (Zimbabwe), 1898–1923*. London: Fairleigh Dickinson UP, 1980.

Opperman, A. J. P. *The Battle of Majuba*. Johannesburg: Perskor Publishers, 1981.

Pakenham, Thomas. *The Scramble for Africa: White Man's Conquest of the Dark Continent from 1876 to 1912*. New York: Avon Books, 1991.

Parfitt, Tudor. *Journey to the Vanished City: The Search for a Lost Tribe of Israel*. London: Hodder and Stoughton, 1992.

Rotberg, Robert I. *A Political History of Tropical Africa*. New York: Harcourt, Brace & World, Inc, 1965.

———. *The Founder*. Coll. Miles F. Shore. New York: Oxford UP, 1988.

Rudd, Charles Dunell. "The Concession Journey of Charles Dunell Rudd." *In Gold and the Gospel in Mashonaland 1888*. Oppenheimer Series 4. London: Chatto and Windus, 1949.

Samkange, Stanlake. *African Saga: A Brief Introduction to African History*. Nashville: Abingdon Press, 1971.

———. *On Trial for My Country*. African Writers Series 33. London: Heinemann Educational Books Ltd, 1966.

———. *Origins of Rhodesia*. New York: Frederick A. Praeger, 1968.

Stocker, Mary. "The Rudd Concession: A Reappraisal of an Intricate Controversy." *Zimbabwean History* 10 (1979): 1–21.

Thomas, Antony. *Rhodes*. New York: St. Martin's Press, 1996.

Index

124

Shangani, Battle of, 76–77
Shangani River, annihilation of
    Matabele impi, 76–77
Shippard, Sir Sidney, 46–47; about
    rifles, 56; and English breaking faith,
    41; on Matabele Matjaha, 46; urged
    Lobengula to sign Rudd Concession,
    47–48
Social Darwinism, 3, 24–25, 33–34
South Africa, brief history, 9–11
South African Republic, 30
Southern Africa: British Interest in,
    17–21; map of segmentation, 7;
    political map, 27; power struggle, 9
steamboat, vague description, 95–96
steam engine, 40
steam locomotive, 40
Suez Canal: British purchase
    controlling interest, 19; completion
    of, 18–19
Suez to the North, 23, 26, 66
Swazi king, 41

Tati, attack at, 75
technological advantage of British, 40
territory, defining, 93
Thomas, Antony, 25, 45
Thompson, Frances Robert (Frank), 42,
    92; about rifles, 49; bulls and cows
    analogy, 48; fled from Matabele, 62;
    and Lobengula, 61
3 C's, p. 2–3, 25
timeline of events, 63
trade, British control of eastern, 19,
    20
translation and use of metaphor, 101
translator, skills of, 97
Transvaal War (1880), 26
troopers kept gold, 79
"Troubled One," 11
tyrant, overthrow of, 34–35

Ulundi, Battle of, 38

uncontested territory as Royal Charter
    requirement, 86

van Riebeeck, Jan, 9–10
verbal concessions v. written agreement,
    51–52, 101
verbal promises, 49, 104–5; analysis of,
    105–7
Victoria Agreement, 73
Victoria Falls, 30
Victoria incident, 70–76
Viljoen, Johannes, ix
von Bismarck, Otto, 28
Voortrekkers, 15

warfare, justification for, 33
weapons, modern, 38–39, 93–94
weapons, native, 38–39
weapons, natives not trained, 94
weapons and money for more, 55
Western powers, aid from, x
Wheatcroft, Geoffrey, 25
white minority colonial population,
    114
Williams, Ralph, 67
Wilson, Major Allan and Victoria
    Column, 74
Witwatersrand, 26
world trade routes in the 1880s, 18
written agreement v. verbal concessions,
    51–52, 101

ZANU PF party, ix, x–xi, 111, 115
Zimbabwe: indigenization effort, viii;
    name change, 80
Zimbabwe civil war (1966–1979), ix
Zimbabwe in 2007, vii, 111
Zimbabwe Nationalist Liberation Army
    (ZANLA), ix
Zulu and Matabele Warrior Nations
    (Palley), 35
Zulu Clan, 11–14
Zulu warriors, 38